Evaluation: A Tool for Improving HRD Quality

Nancy M. Dixon

University Associates, Inc.
8517 Production Avenue
San Diego, California 92121

in association with

**American Society for
Training and Development**
1630 Duke Street
ASTD Alexandria, Virginia 22313

Copyright © 1990 by University Associates, Inc.
ISBN 0-88390-035-1
Library of Congress Catalog Card Number 90-050401
Printed in the United States of America

Library of Congress Cataloging-in-Publication Data

Dixon, Nancy.
  Evaluation: a tool for improving HRD quality.

  Includes bibliographical references and index.
  1. Employees—Training of—Evaluation.   I. Title.
HF5549.5 T7D558   1990   658.3'124   90-11238
ISBN 0-88390-035-1

Editing:	Marian K. Prokop
Cover and Design:	Paul Bond
Typesetting:	Judy Whalen

This book is printed on acid-free, recycled stock that exceeds the minimum GPO and EPA specifications for recycled paper.

Table of Contents

Introduction

For the last twenty years human resource development (HRD) professionals have been urged to evaluate the results of their efforts. The need for evaluation has been the topic of numerous journal articles and presentations at national conferences. Yet as recently as 1988, a report on forty-five Fortune 500 companies showed that although 100 percent of the organizations used some form of participant reaction form, only 30 percent used measures of learning and only 15 percent used measures of behavior (Brandenburg & Schultz, 1988).

Perhaps the reason HRD professionals do so little evaluation has less to do with technique than with purpose. Establishing an HRD evaluation system in an organization typically begins with an HRD professional expressing a desire to "do something about evaluation" in the organization. When asked what questions he or she hopes the data will answer, the response is a long, thoughtful pause. As often as not, the purpose the evaluation will serve has not been thought through; rather there is a feeling that evaluation is something that "ought to" be done.

The following example of the "ought to" phenomenon occurred several years ago. Corporate HRD had mandated that all sites put performance measures in their courses to determine how much learning had occurred. The instructors spent days constructing and validating measurement tools for the courses. After each course, instructors duly administered the measures and scored the results. The program manager then compiled the results into a monthly report. At first the instructors were enthusiastic about the process; they found that the data could improve their courses.

However, no one seemed to know what to do with the compiled results. Corporate HRD clearly did not want the results sent to them; they only wanted to know the number of courses that now had such measures. Within a few weeks the program manager stopped compiling results. A few weeks after that, many instructors—who had already gotten the improvement benefit out of the measures—stopped scoring them. The measures continued to be administered so that the departmental managers could say that all courses had performance measures, but it became clear to everyone that these measures were not tied to a plan or purpose.

Evaluation data are just that—data. They are important only if used for some purpose. The purpose, when thought through in advance, determines *what is measured* and *what instruments are used* to collect the data.

Evaluation can serve the following three purpose:

1. To improve the design or delivery of learning events;

2. To increase the use of the learning on the job; and

3. To make decisions about learning in the organization.

Each is a valid reason to collect evaluation data. However, a purpose more encompassing and more critical to HRD's current needs would be *to improve the quality of service HRD provides to the organization.*

One lesson that HRD practitioners can learn from manufacturing is that tracking quality part by part does not add up to improving quality. The parts must fit into a total quality plan. This book proposes that HRD professionals focus on the quality of the service they provide the organization, using the tools of evaluation to support improvement.

Chapter 2, which completes Part I, outlines a quality plan for HRD modeled on Juran's (1988) quality planning. Each of the subordinate purposes of evaluation is outlined in this chapter and then is explored more completely in a subsequent section. Part II addresses the purpose of improving the design and delivery of learning events, including a discussion of tools, the process for selecting tools, and the problems involved. Part III addresses the purpose of increasing the use of learning on the job. Again, the process of selecting appropriate tools and the problems involved are outlined. This section also deals with the special issues involved in evaluating management development. Part IV addresses the purpose of making decisions about learning in the organization. The final section, Part V, discusses how to construct a variety of measurement tools (performance demonstrations, objective measures, questionnaires, interviews, and so on) and how to determine the validity of those tools.

The term *learning event* is used in this book to describe any planned experience in which the learning of skills, knowledge, and attitudes are intended as the primary outcomes. It encompasses a wide range of formats through which learning takes place in an organization, such as self-paced programs housed in a library, expert systems used at the work site, action research teams, and internal consultations to help intact work groups with team building, as well as the more typical courses and workshops. In this book, the term *course* designates a subset of learning events in which participants come together for a period of time (ranging from a few hours to a few days) to learn from an instructor about a predefined topic. One of the themes of this book is that HRD professionals need to find new ways to create learning opportunities within organizations. For too long *courses* have been the standard response to learning needs. Thus, at the risk of creating more jargon, it seems important to use the broader term *learning event* to avoid reinforcing the assumption that all learning is conducted in courses or workshops.

THEME 1: HRD professionals need to find new ways to create learning opportunities within organizations.

IMPROVE THE DESIGN AND DELIVERY OF LEARNING EVENTS

Evaluation for the purpose of improving the design and delivery of a learning event (Figure 1-1) involves three kinds of measures. First, information is needed about the extent to which participants actually learned. Learning can be measured in many ways: objective tests, performance demonstrations, simulations, and so on, all of which can be termed *performance measures*. Performance measures can be administered before, embedded within, or administered at the end of learning events. In addition to performance measures, projects completed during or after the learning event can be used to determine the extent to which participants learned.

The second type of measure needed to improve the design and delivery of a learning event is a profile of those who were successful in learning and those who were less successful. Examples of profile characteristics include time in current job, type of job, previous knowledge, and previous experience. Such characteristics can be correlated with the results of performance measures and usage data to provide better information about how to target the learning event. For example, it may be that the length of tenure in management affects both the amount participants learn from an learning event and the extent to which the learning is used on the job. A second theme of this book is that HRD professionals need to collect more data—and more sophisticated kinds of data—to identify clients' needs and to determine if HRD meets their clients' quality requirements. Measuring what each participant gains from each learning event is a step in that direction.

THEME 2: HRD professionals need to collect more data to identify clients' needs.

The third measure needed for improvement is an analysis of the design and delivery of learning events. Was the design carried

Purpose of Evaluation	Measures	Tools
Improve the Design and Delivery of Learning Events	Performance measures of SKA from the learning event	Objective tests Performance observations Product ratings Attitude scales
	Profile of character-istics of learners	Demographic forms Personnel records
	Analysis of design and delivery	Checklist of design elements Checklist of delivery skills
	On-the-job measures of usage and retention of SKA	Observations of performance Anecdotal records Questionnaires Interviews Organizational records
Increase the Use of the Learning on the Job	On-the-job measures of usage and retention of SKA	Observations of performance Anecdotal records Questionnaires Interviews Organizational records
	Identification of organizational and personal con-straints to on-the-job use	Interviews Anecdotal records Questionnaires
Make Decisions About Learning in the Organization	On-the job measures of usage and retention of SKA	Observations of performance Anecdotal records Questionnaires Interviews Organizational records
	Documentation of organizational SKA profiles	Objective tests Observations of performance Product ratings Attitude scales
	Cost/benefit	Cost comparisons Causal model Return on investment
	Benchmarking	Comparisons with other organizations on learning quality and effectiveness

Figure 1-1. Subordinate Purposes of HRD Evaluation

out as intended? For example, if the design calls for the demonstration of a skill followed by two role-play activities for the purpose of practicing the skill, does that really happen during the learning event? The extent to which the original design is implemented can be rated by third-party observers using checklists. Analyzing the delivery of learning events requires an objective critique of the instructor. Observers can rate instructors on content knowledge and on instructional or process skills using checklists either during real learning events or in assessment centers.

INCREASE THE USE OF THE LEARNING ON THE JOB

To increase the use of skills, knowledge, and attitudes (SKA) on the job it is necessary to know the extent of current use and what factors constrain the participants from using the learning. Data on current use can be collected by a variety of means, such as observation, anecdotal records, surveys, interviews, and organizational records. Of critical concern is the timing of the data collection. Skills vary as to how soon they are employed and how long they are retained. For example, welding skills for which a welder receives little feedback on completion of the task tend to diminish over time. On the other hand, word-processing skills for which a typist receives constant feedback improve with use. Thus, the timing and frequency of measuring on-the-job usage are both critical.

An acknowledged dilemma in HRD is that participants may leave a learning event able to perform desired skills but not use these skills on the job because their supervisors or some organizational policies or practices inhibit such use. Although HRD professionals have been very concerned about this situation, little systematic data collection within organizations has been accomplished in order to determine the extent of the problem, the causal relationship, or to assist in changing the situation. A third theme of this book is that it is the HRD professional's responsibility to collect useful data on what constrains participants from using what they have learned. Clearly political considerations must be taken into account when investigating and reporting such constraints. The information is nevertheless integral to HRD's becoming more effective. The time is past when an HRD professional can say, "I did my job; I taught the skills. Now it is up to you, Manager, to see that they are used." It is time for HRD practitioners to accept a new level of responsibility toward their internal customers.

THEME 3: HRD professionals need to collect data on what constrains participants from using what they have learned.

The most important tool for collecting data on constraints is the interview. When sufficient understanding of the constraints has been attained through interviews, surveys and questionnaires can be used to determine the extent of the problems and to correlate constraints to appropriate business indicators to determine their significance.

MAKE DECISIONS ABOUT LEARNING IN THE ORGANIZATION

Given limited budgets, HRD professionals must decide which learning events to continue, which to expand, and which to discontinue. They also must decide what new needs or new customers to address. Data about on-the-job usage of learning, rather than performance measures collected at the end of the learning event, are more pertinent for use in making these decisions.

The profile data discussed earlier are also pertinent to these decisions. Profile data can reveal errors in HRD's service to the organization in the interest of continuous improvement.

In addition, it is necessary to analyze the cost of the learning event and its benefit to the organization. Cost is calculated from the direct and indirect costs of providing learning events, including participant time and loss of production. The benefit to the organization is most often thought of as profit or savings expressed in dollars. However, many benefits valued by the organization are beyond those measurable in dollars (Brinkerhoff, 1987). For example, organizations value safety, their reputation in the community, and a positive image that allows them to recruit outstanding college graduates. To accurately determine the costs and benefits, one must include the cost or loss of benefit in ignoring a problem or skill deficit.

Benchmarking allows HRD professionals to compare their effectiveness to their counterparts in other organizations in terms of key indicators. Benchmarks might include the ratio of delivery time versus consulting time for trainers, the percentage of time spent on needs assessment versus design, and the number of HRD personnel.

Finally, decisions about organizational learning are assisted by documentation of the skills, knowledge, and attitudes that exist within the organization. This information provides a fundamental measure of HRD's effectiveness.

Quality Planning for HRD

In many organizations, HRD professionals have successfully taught quality concepts to both managers and employees to help organizations to become more productive and competitive. Human resource development, however, has been less diligent in applying these same concepts to itself. Current evaluation practices in HRD can be likened to the early practices of quality control in manufacturing: they focus narrowly on the defects in the product rather than taking a broader concept of quality, such as conformance to customer requirements.

Evaluation of HRD is not an end in itself; rather, evaluation processes—such as needs assessment, performance measures of learning, and measures of usage on the job—are more effectively used as tools within a total plan for HRD quality. This chapter offers a process for HRD quality planning using Juran's (1988) model. The steps in the model are provided here as an illustration rather than as a formula. It would be preferable for an HRD department to use the same process for internal quality planning that is being used in the organization as a whole.

Figure 2-1 diagrams the steps in Juran's model as modified to apply to HRD. Each numbered step represents a process that results in an output, which then becomes the input to the next process, which again has an output.

The first input into the quality planning process is the existing or redefined product and process. *Product* is a generic term that implies either goods or service. Clearly, HRD is in the business of

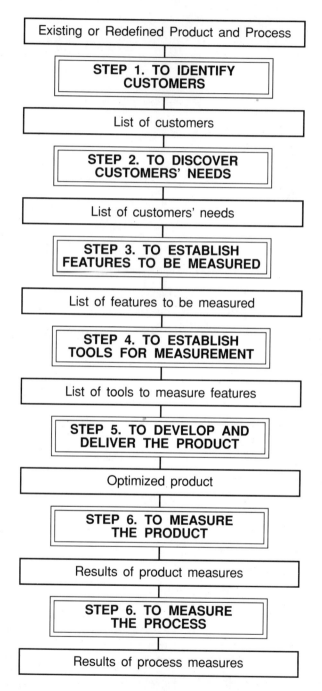

Figure 2-1. Steps in the HRD Quality-Planning Process

service to the organization, as are many other staff functions. As Lawton (1989) notes, it is helpful for a service organization to treat service as a tangible product. Too often, service providers regard their output as a series of activities rather than as specific outcomes. However, activities are intangible and, therefore, are very difficult to measure.

Like other service organizations, HRD tends to regard its service as one of providing activities. Such activities include scheduled courses that target specific functions and levels within the organization as well as custom-designed courses that target a specific problem and are taught only once or twice.

An important first task in the HRD quality process is to redefine the product in terms of an outcome rather than an activity. The desired outcome might include any or all of the following aspects:

- A skilled and knowledgeable work force;
- Employees capable of continual learning;
- Identification and resolution of organizational problems;
- A specific organizational change; or
- An organization that has learned how to engage in continuing change.

If the HRD practitioner identifies a number of products, it becomes important to use the Pareto principle to determine the vital products. In his glossary, Juran (1988, p. 331) defines the Pareto principle as "the phenomenon whereby, in any population that contributes to a common effect, a relative few of the contributors account for the bulk of the effect."

STEP ONE: TO IDENTIFY CUSTOMERS

Customers come in two forms, internal and external. As a department within an organization, most of HRD's customers are internal. However, in some organizations, HRD also provides courses that are marketed to external clients, such as a computer company that sells software training to equipment purchasers. Human resource development consulting firms that market courses to organizations primarily have external customers.

A customer is anyone who is affected by the product or its development. A flow chart of the process used to create the existing product can help to identify the customers involved. For example, Figure 2-2 (pages 14 and 15) diagrams a simplified process for producing courses. A flow chart of the process would vary for each HRD department, particularly if HRD has redefined its product as something other than courses.

As shown in Figure 2-2, each of the following is a customer at a certain point: line managers, participants (internal and external), and upper management. These customers are in addition to the internal relationships within the department that also can be viewed as customer relationships, such as with graphics or printing. The exercise of creating a detailed flow chart can reveal customers that the HRD department had not taken into consideration.

Not all customers are of equal importance. Using the Pareto principle of 80/20, the hotel industry defines the "useful many" to be travelers who stay at the hotel once or twice a year. The "vital few" are the planners of conventions who buy large blocks of rooms well in advance.

The question of identifying the vital few customers in HRD is critical. Traditionally, HRD has considered participants in courses to be its most important customers and has focused its quality measures on them through the use of participant reaction forms. Applying the Pareto principle, however, one can think of participants as the useful many and upper management as the vital few.

The argument for classifying upper management as a vital customer is not unlike the classification used in the hotel illustration. Participants do not pay for courses. In fact, participants may be reluctant users of the service, sometimes attending only because a course is required by management. Either through cost centers, profit centers, or as overhead, upper management pays for courses. When programs are cut, management does the cutting, not the participants. Similarly, the content of training is specified by line managers. Although participants often select which programs to attend, line management identifies what should be offered through the needs assessment process or through the identification of specific problems.

The output of identifying customers is a list of customers classified into the vital few and the useful many. Figure 2-3 (page 16) displays the input for this step, the two processes, and the output, including examples of potential HRD customers.

STEP TWO: TO DISCOVER CUSTOMERS' NEEDS

The process of discovering customer needs results in a list of those needs. To deal with that list, it is useful to distinguish between *stated needs* and *real needs*. Juran (1988) uses the example of a customer whose stated need is a new television but whose real need may be entertainment, or a customer whose stated need is an automobile but whose real need may be transportation. The purpose of the process of discovering customer needs is to go beyond stated needs to try to understand the real need on which the stated need is based.

Typically, HRD has used needs assessment instruments as its primary tool for discovering customer needs. Unfortunately, these instruments too often capture only stated needs. To get at real needs, HRD practitioners must communicate extensively with the customer.

Going into great depth with every customer is an impossibility; priorities must be set. To understand thoroughly the needs of the vital few, the HRD professional needs to spend extensive time with these people on a one-to-one basis. Data on the useful many can be collected through less personal and less time-consuming approaches, such as surveys.

If upper management is among the vital few, the challenge to HRD professionals is to gain enough access to that level to determine the real learning needs of the organization. In the past, HRD

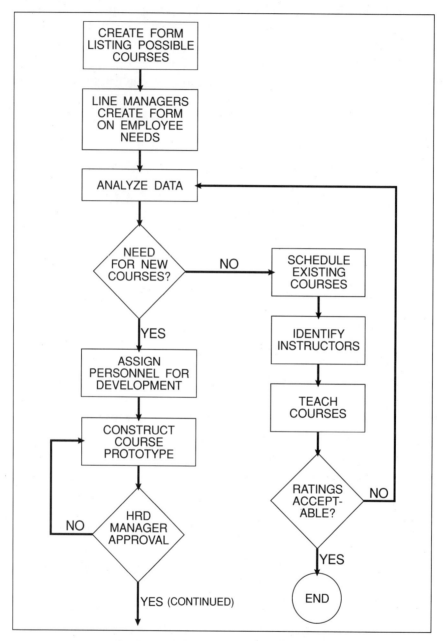

**Figure 2-2. Sample Flow Chart Used to Identify
Customers for the Existing Product**

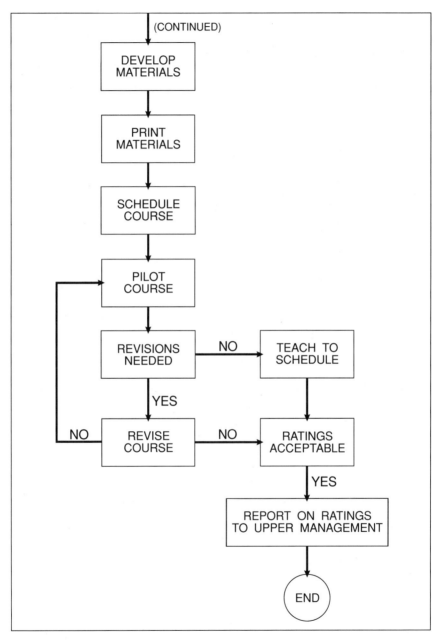

Figure 2-2 (continued). Sample Flow Chart Used to Identify Customers for the Existing Product

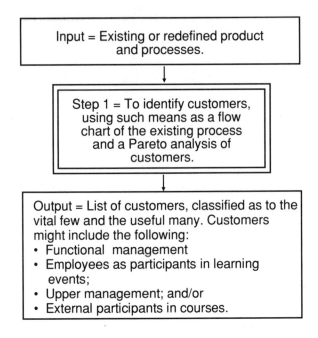

Figure 2-3. Step One in HRD Quality Planning

professionals often felt that meeting the stated needs of upper management was sufficient. Although this strategy can work for the short term, it does not provide the data HRD needs to improve its own quality.

Access to management can be a problem at mid-management levels as well. Many HRD departments have unspoken norms against bothering management. Without adequate communication with its customers, courses may be created that are only marginally relevant. If this situation continues for too long in an organization, HRD is seen as a place employees go for a little "rest and relaxation," rather than as a service critical to the success of the organization.

Talking to noncustomers is as important as talking to customers. What individuals or parts of the organization do not use HRD's services? What are their needs? Is there a tendency to be involved with HRD in the first five years of employment and then to stop?

In addition to increased communication, one useful way to discover customer needs is to be one. Human resource development professionals can easily lose touch with the realities faced by employees in other departments. Helping participants to implement what they have learned is one way to close the gap and to spend time in the customer's environment.

When HRD professionals identify customer needs they must listen for more than new topics for courses. The task is also to identify new products and to find new ways to deliver those products. Two examples serve to illustrate the idea of new HRD products and delivery.

One overnight carrier company sends a videotape to each location daily, providing an update on the organization's business indicators and including a brief lesson on a topic such as customer relations. This unique approach provides consistent reinforcement for subjects that would otherwise be forgotten in the hustle of daily activity. Consistent reinforcement is more effective than the traditional approach of bringing customer service representatives together once a year for a three-day course in customer relations.

A second example is pay-for-skill compensation systems. In these systems, work-team members can increase their pay by learning to use a new piece of equipment or by acquiring skills (such as basic electrical principles) or even community skills (such as CPR). Employees may learn the new skills through individual self-paced modules, through working with a training facilitator, or simply through taking a test to demonstrate knowledge and capability.

When HRD professionals consider their product to be courses, they listen for customer needs that are potential topics for courses. When they define their product more broadly, they listen for new ways to serve the organization's learning needs.

Figure 2-4 illustrates the second step in this process. Several processes lead to the output, which is a list of customer needs classified as to criticality. Although the list of needs that would result is unique to each organization, several examples are provided.

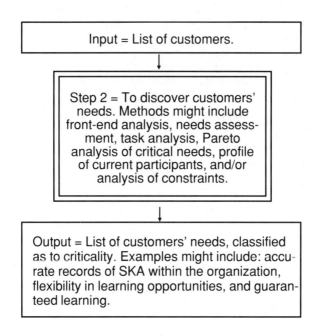

Figure 2-4. Step Two in HRD Quality Planning

STEP THREE: TO ESTABLISH FEATURES TO BE MEASURED

After establishing customer needs, the next step is to determine whether or not those needs are being met. Two elements are important to that end: (1) establishing which features to measure, and (2) developing tools or instruments to collect the data. This step deals with establishing the features and the next deals with the measurement tools.

Juran (1988, p. 70) terms this as the need to determine the "amount of some quality feature which permits evaluation of that feature in numbers." In the automobile industry, a customer need is fuel efficiency; the feature to measure then is miles per gallon. In the airline industry, a customer need is on-time arrival; therefore the feature to measure becomes hours and minutes.

The defined features are used for the following purposes:

1. To determine how well customer needs are being met;

2. To determine how well the product itself performs; and

3. To determine how well the production process works.

The list of features provides a vehicle for communicating with the customer as well as a precise language for communicating internally about product and process performance.

Choosing which feature to measure depends on what has been discovered about customer needs, which in turn depends on how the product is defined. In HRD, if the product is defined as courses, then the appropriate features to measure might be the number of courses, the number of participants in courses, and the cost per participant-day. If HRD's product is defined as a skilled and knowledgeable work force, the feature to measure might be the number of employees who have demonstrated the skills to do their jobs versus the number who have skill deficits. If HRD's product is defined to be a work force able to adapt to changing circumstances, the feature to measure might be the number of employees who have multiple skills, allowing the work force to function in more flexible ways. Figure 2-5 shows the input, the process, and the output of this step.

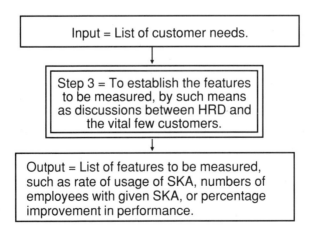

Figure 2-5. Step Three in HRD Quality Planning

STEP FOUR: TO ESTABLISH TOOLS
FOR MEASUREMENT

The input into the process of establishing tools for measurement is a list of features to be measured. Currently, HRD has a number of measurement tools at its disposal. Participant reaction forms provide data on how much a course was enjoyed. Performance measures provide data on how much was actually learned in a course. Measures of usage indicate how much of the learning has been used on the job.

The problem with these measures is twofold. First, they relate only to courses or the application of those courses, not to a broader HRD product. Second, these measures are not a part of a total quality plan that ties them back to customer needs. If HRD accomplishes better and more systematic communication with its customers, atypical needs may result. Such needs are likely to be unique to each customer, so measurement tools also will vary. In the past, human resource development has striven for a standardized product. Dick (1986, p. 6) says that the goal of the instructional designer is "to create an instructional package for the largest possible target population." However, the focus on customers forces most organizations away from standardization toward product differentiation. The time of standardization in HRD products and measurement may be in the past.

Figure 2-6 illustrates the process of establishing tools for measurement.

STEP FIVE: TO DEVELOP AND TO DELIVER
THE PRODUCT

To develop and deliver products, HRD professionals first create a design. The input for designing the product is the list of customer features and the tools that will be used to measure those features. The final design takes into account the customer's needs, HRD's needs and constraints, and information about competitors. The goal

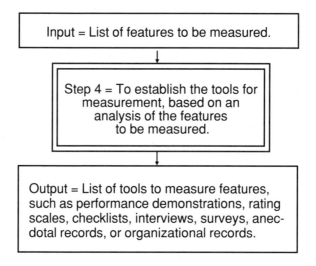

Input = List of features to be measured.

Step 4 = To establish the tools for measurement, based on an analysis of the features to be measured.

Output = List of tools to measure features, such as performance demonstrations, rating scales, checklists, interviews, surveys, anecdotal records, or organizational records.

Figure 2-6. Step Four in HRD Quality Planning

is to optimize the needs of the customer and HRD, while being "best in class" in terms of the competition.

In the second and third steps of this process, the customer's needs were analyzed and the features to be measured were established. However, involvement with the customer does not end here. By including customers as partners in the design process, HRD professionals not only ensure their support but also provide a quality check on the product and process.

One large manufacturing organization launched a massive effort to implement just-in-time inventory processes in each of its plant sites. Corporate Manufacturing Education's responsibility was to teach the skills needed to implement the new process to employees at all levels. Its first step was to set up a series of meetings with plant management to establish the joint goals for the learning, including the features to be measured, the criteria for competence in the courses, the consequences if an employee did not meet the criteria, and such things as schedule, cost, and materials. This lengthy and ongoing dialog with the customer made the effort successful, both in terms of the amount of learning and the support of line management for the learning process.

The needs of HRD must also be considered in the design. Budget, time, or personnel limitations may make it impossible to meet certain customer needs. The design should optimize the combined needs of HRD and the customer. Because HRD professionals tend to have a genuine service orientation—and perhaps because HRD has not always had a secure position within organizations—HRD professionals tend to agree to the impossible when top management asks it of them. For example, management may ask HRD to have a course on line without sufficient time to produce a quality product. In an attempt to be of service, HRD professionals may agree to the request, despite realizing that the product will be of poor quality. The result has often been self-defeating, with both management and HRD recognizing that the product did not meet the goal (Dixon, 1989). Both the customer's needs and HRD's needs must be taken into account in the design.

Finally, good design takes the competition into account. It might seem that an internal HRD department would not have to be concerned with competition. However, in a number of organizations, internal competition has severely impacted HRD.

In one organization, line management's goal was to establish a participative management system throughout the total organization. Rather than involve HRD, line management decided to hire external consultants to provide training for the participative processes. The HRD professionals were seen as too removed from the line operation to be effective, as well as too busy teaching their own courses.

In another case, HRD contracted with an external training organization to develop and deliver a specific program. Subsequently, the external trainers were asked back to consult on related projects begun during the course. Because such requests were seldom made of in-house trainers, it became clear to corporate HRD that the external trainers were meeting a customer need that internal trainers had not been meeting.

An important consideration in the determination of the product features is benchmarking. In 1979, Xerox initiated a process it called competitive benchmarking. As the label implies, benchmarking was done at first against competitors. However, it was gradually understood that benchmarking needed to be done against anyone who had superior practices. The focus of benchmarking is twofold: on results and on the process. In addition to providing targets, benchmarking identifies practices that have been successful elsewhere, which therefore are more likely to be accepted as possible.

In 1986, Motorola spearheaded an HRD benchmarking effort that involved Hitachi, Intel, Ericcson, Matsushita, Northern Telecom, Philips, Hewlett-Packard, and NEC. Benchmarked areas included:

- Training's role in the development of cell managers (robotics);
- Training's role in the implementation of manufacturing equipment and processes;
- Curricula development, including types of training, populations served, and results;
- Course design;
- Implementation of training goals; and
- Training services offered.

Another recent effort involved a group of HRD managers from seven organizations (DEC, Dictaphone, Hewlett-Packard, NCR, Texas Instruments, 3M, and Xerox), who joined to benchmark three HRD functions: service training, service documentation, and customer training. This was a landmark HRD benchmarking effort. Twenty-two pages of measurement items were defined to provide ways of looking at organizations, people, development processes, delivery processes, quality measurements, and productivity measurements. This effort resulted in organizational profiles as well as "best-in-class" profiles.

With a proper design that derives from discussions with the customer, an analysis of HRD needs, and benchmarking, the HRD department is able to develop and deliver an optimized product (Figure 2-7).

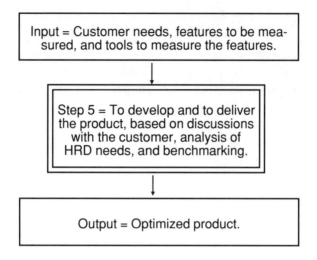

Figure 2-7. Step Five in HRD Quality Planning

STEP SIX: TO MEASURE THE PRODUCT

The next step is to use measurement tools to determine if the product meets the quality goals established for it in the planning process and to use that information to make whatever changes are needed to improve the product. Measuring the product and measuring the process are a part of continuous improvement.

The data are also part of an ongoing dialog with the customer. One reason HRD professionals give for not spending energy on evaluation is that management is not interested in the results. To some extent, management's lack of interest is a result of the choice of features to be measured. When managers help to define the features to be measured, the results have meaning and import to them.

Figure 2-8 shows the input of the optimized product, the process of measuring the product, and the output of the results of the measures.

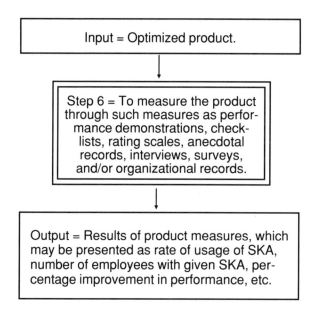

Figure 2-8. Step Six in HRD Quality Planning

STEP SEVEN: TO MEASURE THE PROCESS

The final step is examining or measuring the process itself. In this step both internal and external information are important. The tools to measure HRD's internal process are those related to learning and usage. Improving the product and the process requires information on retention and information on constraints on usage. Costs of developing and delivering the product need to be calculated. Benchmarking data constitute the external measures.

Much of the process data is for HRD's internal use. However, the data on constraints must be shared with others if changes are to be made. The HRD professionals are not responsible for removing constraints to usage; they are, however, responsible for providing information to those who can make such changes and thereby improve the process. Figure 2-9 lists possible results of these measures.

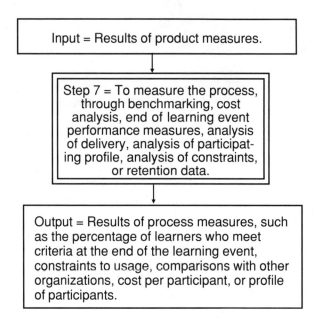

Figure 2-9. Step Seven in HRD Quality Planning

Thus, HRD quality planning can be seen as an adaptation of Juran's model of planning for quality. This concludes Part I, which discussed how evaluation can improve HRD quality. Part II will examine the broad purpose of improving the design and delivery of a learning event.

3

The Dangers of Using Participant Reaction Forms

Nearly all HRD departments evaluate the programs they provide in an effort to improve those programs. The vast majority of such evaluations consist of some type of participant reaction form administered at the end of the learning event. Such forms typically ask participants their opinions about the instructor, the extent to which the objectives were met, the relevance of the content, and the quality of the audiovisual materials, printed materials, and facilities. Although such forms are used widely, it is questionable whether the data they provide are useful in improving the design and delivery of a learning event.

The following four types of measures can be used to improve the design and delivery of learning events:

1. Performance measures of skills, knowledge, and attitudes;

2. Profile of the characteristics of the learners;

3. Analysis of the design and delivery; and

4. On-the-job measures of usage and retention.

Each of these measures will be discussed in some depth. However, given the popularity of participant reaction forms, this chapter first addresses the problems associated with their use.

THREE ASSUMPTIONS ABOUT THE PERCEPTIONS OF PARTICIPANTS

Many HRD professionals make the following three assumptions about the perceptions of participants who are involved in learning events:

1. Participants are able to make accurate judgments about how much they have learned;
2. Participants learn more from courses they enjoy; and
3. Participants learn more from instructors they perceive to be skillful.

On the basis of these assumptions, participant reaction forms are designed and administered, results are tallied, and decisions are made about how to improve the courses. Unfortunately, studies of the relationship between actual learning achieved in a course and how participants complete reaction forms indicate that such a relationship is either very small or nonexistent (Clement, 1982; Israelite, 1983; King, 1982).

A 1990 study supports this conclusion (Dixon, 1990). Over 1,400 employees in a large manufacturing organization participated in one of three courses related to the implementation of a new manufacturing process. The amount of actual learning by each participant was determined by performance measures administered at the end of each course. The performance measures were based on course objectives and had gone through an extensive validation process. Participants also completed postcourse forms that asked them to rate the following items on a one-to-seven scale:

1. Amount of new information learned;
2. Enjoyment of session;
3. Instructor qualifications;
4. Skill of instructor;
5. Instructor knowledge; and
6. Instructor preparation.

Results of the performance measures were correlated with each participant's perceptions. For the first variable, "amount of new information learned," correlations ranged from -.07 to -.18, indicating no significant relationship between how much participants said they learned and how well they actually did on the performance measure.

This finding is puzzling and uncomfortable. Instructors have long believed that they could rely on participants' perceptions to guide the changes needed in courses. From correlation data, it is not possible to draw definite conclusions about why there is no relationship. Several possible reasons that might explain this finding are presented in the paragraphs that follow.

One hypothesis is that participants do not really know whether they have learned the new material without testing themselves in some way. Most people can recall a time when they read something that they thought they understood—until they tried to explain it to a friend and realized they did not really understand it. It is possible that without some way to test out knowledge or skills, participants are not aware of how much they have or have not learned.

A second hypothesis to explain the lack of relationship is that participants do indeed know whether they have learned, but that they do not mark the forms accordingly. For example, they may be aware that they did not learn much but know that they like the instructor and want to reward him or her. Conversely, they may dislike the instructor and mark the form to reflect that feeling even though they are aware they did learn.

A third possibility is that participants may have come to a course assuming that they will learn very little. If they gain something of value, they may rate the course highly even if that learning falls short of the course objectives from which the performance measures were derived.

Regardless of the explanation, it seems clear that the responses on the participant reaction form in this study were not a good indicator of whether participants learned; more accurate data would be needed to guide improvements.

In the same study, the second factor on the participant reaction form was "enjoyment" (Dixon, 1990). Again the individual's response on the participant reaction form was correlated with that individual's actual score on the performance measure. These correlations also were not significant (-.02 to .07). These data indicate no relationship between how much participants said they enjoyed the course and how much they learned.

Given the long-standing assumption in the training community that learning and enjoyment are related, this result is equally disconcerting. What these data seem to say is that any one of the following relationships between learning and enjoyment can exist:

1. A participant may not enjoy a course and not learn from it;

2. A participant may both enjoy the course and learn from it;

3. A participant may enjoy a course but not learn from it; or

4. A participant may not enjoy the course and still learn from it.

The first two items restate commonly held beliefs. The third and fourth statements make the responses from participant reaction forms questionable as data to guide improvement. If learning and enjoyment are not related, then data on how much participants enjoyed a course cannot be used to improve learning.

The final four factors in this study (Dixon, 1990) all related to the instructor. These ratings also were correlated with participants' actual scores on performance measures. Results indicated no significant relationship (.05 to -.16) between how the instructor was perceived and how much participants actually learned.

Again, because statistical data give only figures and not explanations, it is necessary to try to understand why such a result might occur. Several explanations seem possible. One hypothesis is that participants could not judge the instructors accurately; they could not say whether or not the instructors were skillful or knowledgeable. This interpretation is somewhat logical, because participants are unlikely to be enrolled in a course if they know the subject matter. A second explanation is that there is no relationship between the skills, knowledge, and attitude of the instructor and how well participants learn; this explanation proposes that, in fact, participant learning is related to something other than instructor skill. A third explanation is that participants are able to judge instructors accurately, but choose to mark the reaction form based on other factors, such as how much they like the instructor. Again, although it is not possible to say which of these explanations is true from the correlations, it is clear that the participants' opinions of the instructor in this study were not an indication of how much they learned.

These data call into question the assumption that trainers can rely on the responses of participants to make course improvements; however, a case could be made that participants' responses still might be useful. The remainder of this chapter argues that not only do participant reaction forms fail to provide useful information, but contends that using them as the exclusive source of evaluation data can actually be detrimental to program improvement. Three major problems can result from the use of participant reaction forms as the exclusive source of evaluation data:

1. The expectation that learning events will be entertaining;

2. Faulty instructional-design decisions; and

3. The perception of learning as passive rather than active.

THE EXPECTATION THAT LEARNING EVENTS WILL BE ENTERTAINING

Figure 3-1 depicts a positive-feedback loop that can develop as a result of relying on participant reaction forms for evaluation. It illustrates that if participants enjoyed the course and left with a good feeling about the instructor, they would give the instructor high ratings.

Ratings on participant reaction forms often are a major factor in determining the reward an instructor receives from the organization. For external consultants, high ratings mean the renewal of

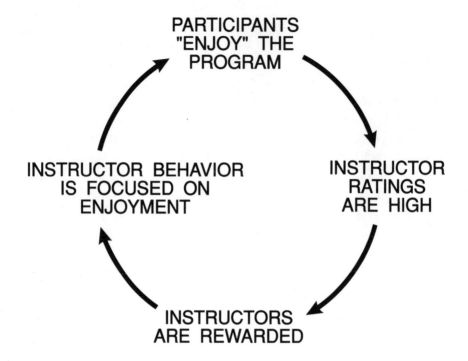

**Figure 3-1. Positive-Feedback Loop Resulting
from Reliance on Participant Reaction Forms**

a contract; for internal trainers, high ratings mean good performance reviews or commendations from their managers. When instructors are rewarded for high ratings and are punished for low ratings, they tend to modify their behavior to ensure participant enjoyment. As courses become more entertaining, the standard by which participants evaluate the courses escalates. This positive-feedback loop produces a rising trend toward entertaining courses. If, as the data indicate, no relationship exists between enjoyment and learning, an emphasis on enjoyment may prevent instructors from focusing on behaviors that could increase learning.

The data described previously also support the existence of a positive-feedback loop that places increasing importance on enjoyment. This feedback loop predicts a significant correlation between how much participants enjoy the learning and how highly they rate the instructors. This correlation was computed using the data from the manufacturing study (Dixon, 1990). The results support the premise of the feedback loop; significant correlations (ranging from .18 to .60) accounted for up to 36 percent of the variance between enjoyment and instructor ratings. These data lend support to the idea that participant enjoyment may influence how highly participants rate instructors.

The reason that such a correlation might exist is understandable. Experienced trainers learn behaviors that earn them high ratings on participant reaction forms. To a large extent, high ratings are a function of being personable, keeping the energy in the room at a high level, and keeping things moving. Despite the fact that trainers are committed to participants' learning, this commitment often conflicts with the need to keep their ratings up by being entertaining. Trainers, like other employees in the corporate setting, tend to place more emphasis on the activities whereby they are measured and rewarded.

A focus on enjoyment conflicts with the reality that learning often is an uncomfortable activity. "Having learned" is pleasurable; the process of learning often is not. As Piaget (Sund, 1976) has shown, much learning involves altering an existing idea or schema that the individual has constructed in his or her own mind. This alteration often entails a period of confusion, during which the existing schema is in doubt and the new construction is not yet in place. The more complex the idea being learned, the longer the period of confusion that must be tolerated. When learning involves the changing of values and attitudes, as much of management development does, the period of dissonance is even more stressful. This additional stress occurs because such learning affects the identity of the individual more so than the less personal learning involved in abstract concepts. Lewin (1951) uses the term "unfreezing" to describe the act of unlearning an existing concept or behavior. Unfreezing leaves the learner feeling vulnerable and dependent until a new attitude is incorporated or refrozen. Instructors must often make the choice between teaching simple ideas in a pleasurable way, thus insuring themselves high ratings, or teaching complex ideas that will generate uncertainty and confusion in the participants, thereby risking lower ratings on participant reaction forms.

The desire to be liked by participants handicaps an instructor in other ways as well. The instructor's effectiveness in challenging incorrect or shallow thinking by the participants is lessened. For example, instructors rarely tell participants that their comments or answers are incorrect. The accepted practice is to offer an alternative for the participant "to think about," or for the instructor to somehow expand on the participant's comment until it becomes correct. However, research (Soar, 1982) shows that when learners receive positive feedback on all the answers they give, they become less discriminating in their own thinking and exercise less critical thought before offering comments. Again, the positive-feedback loop may impair the learning process.

FAULTY INSTRUCTIONAL-DESIGN DECISIONS

The second problem that can result from the use of participant reaction forms is faulty instructional design decisions. Questionnaires and surveys that result in accurate information are difficult to design. One of the most common mistakes inexperienced designers make is to ask questions about which the respondent has insufficient knowledge. The art of questionnaire design is to ask those questions about which the respondent can give an *informed* response. Typical participant reaction forms ask questions such as the following:

- Were the course objectives met?
- How clear were the course materials?
- Was sufficient practice time allocated for learning new behaviors?
- Was the course of appropriate length?

Unless the participant happens to be an expert in the subject matter or in instructional design, he or she will have incomplete criteria upon which to make such decisions.

The concept of *transfer of skills* illustrates the problem of respondents being asked questions that are more appropriately answered by instructional designers. The number of practice sessions needed to learn (transfer) a skill well enough to use it on the job depends on four factors: difficulty, importance, amount of feedback, and frequency of use. (These factors are described more completely in Chapter 9). Some tasks are very complex: they have several items or concepts to be considered at one time, they are infrequently performed on the job, and they require correct performance the first time they are accomplished. An example of such a task might be repairing a complex piece of computer equipment. To retain performance above the 90 percent level for as long as eighteen weeks, the skill would need to be learned in a series of three to five training sessions with correct performance achieved by the end of each. If only a single training session were provided, the individual could be expected retain the information for only two weeks without performing and still perform at above the 90-percent level. When participants are asked to evaluate whether or not sufficient time was provided for skill practice, the only basis they have for making that decision is whether or not they have just accomplished the task successfully. Success or failure in that one instance is insufficient data with which to make the judgment, yet their collective response on the form may result in a decision to limit practice to one session.

A second example, one familiar to management instructors, is the use of role play. Participants whose learning style leans more toward the abstract than the concrete generally feel uncomfortable with role play, and typically they will indicate on participant reaction forms that the role play in the session was a waste of time. Yet instructional designers know that participants are unlikely to learn interpersonal skills by reading or hearing about them; most must practice the skills and receive feedback if they are to grasp the new concepts fully.

The problems associated with making design decisions based on participant perception are as true for open-ended questions as they are for multiple-choice or rated items. Questions that ask what participants like best and least also yield data that often are based on heartfelt, but uninformed, opinion.

THE PERCEPTION OF LEARNING AS PASSIVE RATHER THAN ACTIVE

This third problem reflects the widely held assumption that it is the instructor's responsibility to ensure that learning occurs. The participant is perceived as passive, someone to be acted on. Participant reaction forms reinforce this concept by asking questions about the instructor's performance, the course design, and the site—but not about the participant's own effort or behavior.

However, learning is not a passive but an active process. Even when the learning event takes the form of a lecture, in which learning appears to be passive, participants must act internally. They need to think of examples of the concept, relate the information to what they already know, check themselves for understanding, and so on. Without such active processing, participants quickly forget what was presented. When the learning is skill based or when it requires participants to change or examine self-concepts, the participants must be even more active. After years of filling out reaction forms, participants in many organizations have become polished at critiques of courses, as the following actual comments attest:

- It was a little slow from 2 to 4 o'clock.
- The instructor should have provided more relevant examples; all the ones given were from materials handling.
- Could have been better organized.

These comments reveal little awareness that participants are responsible for asking for what they need to learn, for sharing what happens in the classroom, or for working actively at learning. Such comments liken the instructor to an Olympic performer and the participants to judges who hold up cards to rate the performance.

Organizations measure those things that are considered to be important to allow those involved to correct their processes. One by-product is that the evaluation itself works like a pointer to tell others what the organization regards as important. However, participant reaction forms point neither to the amount of effort made by learners nor to the learning gains that resulted; they measure only the efforts of the instructor/designer. The act of filling out the form teaches participants that the active involvement of the instructor, not the participant, is most important in the training process.

To review, use of performance evaluation forms can lead to three negative outcomes: (1) the generation of a positive-feedback loop that encourages instructors to entertain rather than to focus on participant learning; (2) the risk of making faulty design decisions based on participant feedback; and (3) the implication to the participants that learning is passive. For these reasons, the detrimental effects of using participant reaction forms may outweigh any benefits. Clearly, using participant reaction forms as the only evaluation is most detrimental. Coupled with other forms of evaluation, data from participant reaction forms are less harmful.

Time Frames for Measuring Learning

Four types of measures are needed to improve the design and delivery of learning events:

1. Performance measures of skills, knowledge, and attitudes;
2. Profile of the characteristics of the learners;
3. Analysis of the design and delivery; and
4. On-the-job measures of usage and retention of skills, knowledge, and attitudes.

Chapters 4, 5, and 6 deal with aspects of the first of these, performance measures. The remaining topics are covered in later chapters.

PERFORMANCE MEASURES

Performance measures are tools that measure the actual skills, knowledge, and attitudes of participants in learning events—as opposed to the participants' perceptions of those skills, knowledge, and attitudes. The term is used here generically to refer to any of the different tools available. Such tools range from paper-and-pencil tests to demonstrations of skills in real situations. When using performance measures, three important considerations are (1) when and how often the measures are administered; (2) which methods are employed; and (3) what problems are associated with their introduction and implementation. Chapter 4 deals with the first of these considerations.

TIME FRAMES OF PERFORMANCE MEASURES

Performance measures can be categorized as to their *time frames*, the "when and how often" of their use. Time frames for measuring learning include prerequisite measures, premeasures, embedded measures, postmeasures, measures of usage, and measures of retention (see Figure 4-1).

Measure	When Applied	Answers the Question	Purpose
Prerequisite Measures	Before the learning event	Does the participant have the background knowledge needed to learn. . .?	• To create a homogeneous group • To guide the design of a learning event
Premeasures	Before the learning event	Does the participant already know. . .?	• To determine if the participant needs to be involved in a specific learning event • To tailor the content to a specific population • To compute the learning gain from pretest to posttest • To motivate the participant to learn
Embedded Measures	During the learning event	Has the participant learned this portion of. . .?	• To determine if the participant has mastered a concept that is prerequisite to further learning

Figure 4-1. Time Frames for Performance Measures

Measure	When Applied	Answers the Question	Purpose
Embedded Measures (continued)			• To obtain an accurate measure of learning when individuals participate in only select portions of the learning event
Postmeasures	End of the learning event	Has the participant learned all of the. . .?	• To compute the learning gain from pretest to posttest • To determine which participants need assistance to meet minimum criteria • To construct and maintain an accurate organizational record of skills and knowledge • To certify employees to meet regulations
Measures of Usage	After the learning event	To what extent has the participant used. . . on the job?	• To increase the usage by: - identifying constraints to usage - identifying ways to improve the learning event • To provide data with which to make decisions about learning in the organization
Measures of Retention	After the learning event	For what length of time can the participant accurately perform. . .?	• To improve the learning event • To determine the point at which relearning is needed

Figure 4-1 (continued). Time Frames for Performance Measures

Prerequisite Measures

Prerequisite measures are administered to determine whether or not the participant has the knowledge and skills needed to benefit from the upcoming learning event. For example, a prerequisite measure of basic electronics might be administered before a course on repairing a computer. Members of a quality circle who have decided to teach themselves about statistical process control may need to first determine if they all have the prerequisite knowledge of algebra. An employee starting a computer-assisted instruction program in Fortran II may need to know if he or she has mastered the knowledge in Fortran I. The *content* measured by the prerequisite measure is a different set of skills, knowledge, and attitudes than that planned for the learning event.

Prerequisite measures serve several purposes. First, they can help assure homogeneity among learners by screening out those who do not have the necessary skills or knowledge. If the information is used for this purpose, the prerequisite measure should be administered well in advance of a group learning event. It is costly and demoralizing for individuals to rearrange their schedules in order to participate in an event, only to find out after they arrive that they lack needed background information.

Second, prerequisite measures can establish the baseline knowledge of a specific population, thus guiding the design of the learning event. If, for example, several members of the quality circle are discovered not to remember enough algebra, a refresher course may be made available, or a review of algebra might be incorporated into the design of the learning event. The first use of prerequisite measures adjusts the population; the second use adjusts the content.

In one situation, engineers were trained to use a software package that simulated a manufacturing process. The instructor believed that participants coming into the course needed previous computer experience to be able to do well. However, analysis of the end-of-course data showed that participants who had no computer experience did as well as those who had computer experience. In this situation, the prerequisite measure allowed the designer to collect sufficient data to eliminate computer experience as a prerequisite. For the many learning events that require only general knowledge, no prerequisites measures need be administered.

Premeasures

The second time-related measure is the *premeasure*, often called a *pretest*. The term premeasure is used here rather than pretest to avoid the connotations of paper-and-pencil measures. Premeasures can take the form of technical demonstrations, role plays, surveys of attitudes, and so on. As with the prerequisite measure, this measure is administered before the learning event occurs. It differs from the prerequisite measure in that the skills, knowledge, and attitudes assessed in the premeasure are the same as those planned for the upcoming learning event, whereas the content of the prerequisite measure differs from that of the learning event.

Premeasures can serve several purposes. One purpose is to determine whether it is necessary for a particular participant to take part in the learning event. For example, employees interested in learning about problem solving through a self-paced print package could take premeasures that would tell them how much they already know. These employees then could choose to complete only some portion of the package or could choose a different package altogether. Administering the premeasure at the beginning of the learning event is acceptable in some situations, such as the case of the self-paced print package. In other situations, such as when an employee must travel to a central place for a course, it is more logical to administer the premeasure in advance of the course itself.

A second purpose for the premeasure is to allow the instructor to tailor the content to a particular individual or group. For example, an internal consultant who plans to work with a team to improve meeting skills might collect information on the group's current meeting skills using an observation checklist. This would allow the consultant to know which areas to emphasize. In order to accomplish this purpose, the premeasure must be administered far enough in advance of the learning event to allow needed changes to be made.

A third purpose of premeasures is to calculate the gain between premeasures and postmeasures. For this function, the premeasures and postmeasures must be carefully constructed to cover the same content and to be equivalent in difficulty. (Chapter 20 provides instructions on how to compute difficulty for test items.) If premeasures are used in scheduled courses that are conducted often, it may be helpful to administer premeasures at first to establish baseline data; then, if it appears that the scores vary little from group to group, premeasures could be dropped.

Data showing gains can be useful in the design stage of a program to provide information for revision, but generally are less effective for demonstrating the value of a program to others. It is far more persuasive to show that 90 percent of the participants met the minimum criteria established for a learning event than to show a 25-percent gain between premeasures and postmeasures. There are situations, however, in which minimum criteria cannot be used. For example, if the learning event is meant to persuade managers to increase the frequency with which they involve employees in problem solving, data showing gains correlated to the number of such sessions are clearly more relevant.

When it is unlikely that participants already have the knowledge encompassed in the learning event, a premeasure is unnecessary; zero knowledge can be assumed. For example, if a new software program has just been released, it is superfluous to put participants through a demonstration to prove that they cannot implement it. In many situations a simple question to participants— such as, "Have you used this particular database?"—provides adequate information without the formality of a premeasure.

A fourth purpose in using premeasures is to motivate the learner. For example, participants can experience an *unfreezing* when confronted with data showing them to be less knowledgeable or skillful than they thought. Unfreezing can result in an openness to learning. This technique is often exercised in management development, using questionnaires completed by employees or peers. However, evidence indicates that premeasures also can have demotivating effects on learners. Bunker and Cohen (1977) have shown that under certain circumstances, a premeasure may cause learners to be so discouraged that they learn less than if the premeasure had not been administered; they found this to be particularly true of poorer learners.

Thus the question of whether or not to use premeasures has no simple answer; many considerations need to be taken into account in making the decision.

Embedded Measures

Embedded measures are performance measures that are administered periodically during a learning event as opposed to an encompassing measure at the end of the event. Such periodic measures are helpful when it is important for participants to have mastered a particular concept that will be prerequisite to the next concept. It is also beneficial to use embedded measures if the learning event is lengthy or if it covers multiple, unrelated topics. Finally, if the learning event is designed in such a way that not all participants take part in the entire event, then embedded measures covering each portion are more helpful to the designer than a single postmeasure.

Postmeasures

Postmeasures are administered at the end of a learning event to determine the extent of learning that occurred during the event. The more common term, *posttest*, is avoided here because it tends to imply a paper-and-pencil test rather than to describe the range of measures that can and should be used to measure learning. (The next chapter provides a discussion of the types of postmeasures to use in various situations.)

The most common purpose of postmeasures has already been discussed in the section on premeasures, that is, to compute the gain in learning in order to improve the learning event or to inform others of the value of the learning event.

A second purpose in gathering such information is to determine which participants still need help in gaining skills, knowledge, and attitudes. If this is the intent of postmeasures, then a process needs to be in place to assist those who have not yet met the minimum criteria. Remediation is simplified by tying the postmeasure to specific objectives, making it possible to know the section(s) of the learning on which the participant needs help.

A third purpose of postmeasures is to maintain an organizational record of the skills and knowledge that employees have gained. Such a record is considerably different from the typical record of which employees have attended which courses. Records of skills and knowledge can be useful to planners as well as to individual managers, who may need to recruit in-house employees with certain sets of skills and knowledge. A related purpose for postmeasures is to use the data to certify employees when a particular certification is required by external regulators or by organizational policy.

Traditionally, HRD professionals have not considered it their responsibility to ensure that participants exit a learning event with a minimum level of skills, knowledge and attitudes, much less to remediate those who fall short of these criteria. The prevailing attitude has been that participants in a learning event choose how much they will get out of the event. However, in a time of increasing emphasis on quality and on meeting customer needs, this attitude is changing. This change is due in part to the fact that the logic behind the attitude does not hold up. It is inconsistent for HRD to demand the full support of the organization in developing the skills, knowledge, and attitudes vital to the organization's success and then to decline to record or to remediate the failure of participants to meet minimum criteria. Either the content of learning events is vital to the organization or it is merely "nice to have."

Measures of Usage

Measures of usage are administered some time after the learning event to determine the extent to which the skills, knowledge, and attitudes gained therein are actually being used on the job. Again, a wide range of methods can be employed.

Usage data are collected for two major purposes: (1) to find ways to increase the use of the skills, knowledge, and attitudes on the job, and (2) to provide information with which to make decisions about learning in the organization. Usage data answer these kinds of questions:

- How does the learning event itself need to change?

- What kinds of assistance do participants need after they return to work?

- What constrains participants on the job from implementing what they learned?

Measures of Retention

Measures of retention are other measures that are employed after the learning event. These measures determine the accuracy with which the skill is being performed. Many skills decrease in accuracy over time, particularly skills for which task feedback is not available or skills that are practiced infrequently. It is important to determine at what point such skills fall below an acceptable level. The purpose of collecting such data is to improve the learning event. The amount and type of initial practice affects the length of retention. Thus, based on retention data, a learning event may be lengthened or shortened.

A second purpose of retention data is to determine the point at which relearning should occur to maintain skill accuracy. The concept of skill retention is discussed more fully in Chapter 9.

Analyzing Learning Outcomes to Select Appropriate Measurement Tools

TYPES OF PERFORMANCE MEASURES

Three considerations about performance measures are being examined: time frames, types, and problems. This chapter focuses on the types of performance measures and when each is most appropriately employed.

Figure 5-1 outlines tools that can be used to measure learning. Two considerations govern which measure to use in a given situation:

1. Measures should match the type of learning outcome intended for the learning event; and

2. Measures should approximate, as closely as possible, how the skill, knowledge, or attitude will be used on the job.

LEARNING OUTCOMES

Learning outcomes can be classified as motor skills, intellectual skills, verbal information, attitude, and cognitive strategies (Gagné & Briggs, 1979). Gagné and Briggs have outlined specific conditions and processes that facilitate the learning of each type of outcome. Understanding the learning outcome helps the designer of the learning event; this understanding also aids in evaluation because the type of outcome guides the choice of measurement tool.

```
Objective measures
       - true/false
       - multiple choice
       - matching
       - completion

Attitudinal rating scales

Demonstrations of performance
       - simulated work tasks
       - checklists
       - rating scales
       - product quality
         - trainer
         - peers
         - supervisor
         - assessors (assessment center)
       - projects
       - case study
```

Figure 5-1. Performance Measurements

Motor Skills

Motor skills refer to the physical movements that are performed to accomplish purposeful actions. An example of a motor skill is setting up and operating a video camera. An outcome is classified as a motor skill when the motor component of the task is nontrivial. Motor skills are connected to almost every task; however, in many cases they are trivial in relation to the total task. For example, participants in interview training use the motor actions of talking, shaking hands, and so on, but these motor components are not the focus of learning how to interview. In that sense they are trivial to learning the task of interviewing. Other examples of motor skills that are nontrivial include soldering a connection, lifting a heavy weight, or guiding a projectile.

Motor skills need to be measured by demonstrating the performance of simulated work tasks. The demonstration can be judged by checklists, rating scales, or product quality. The previous example of operating a video camera could conceivably employ any one of the three ways to judge the performance, although typically all three are not employed for the same skill. A checklist might be used by an observer to mark off the steps in the operation such as "turned on power," "removed lens cap," and so on. A rating scale might be used to judge how smoothly the zoom action took place. Finally, the quality of the product, the videotape, could be used to judge the extent to which this motor skill was learned. In some cases the process is only important in the early stages of learning a motor skill (for example, in learning to type).

In judging a participant's ability to perform a motor skill, such as operating a video camera, the measure needs to be a demonstration of that skill. It is not appropriate to ask verbal information questions, such as naming the parts of the camera or listing the steps in camera operation.

One of the difficulties in evaluating motor skills is the amount of time it takes a single instructor with a classroom full of participants to make all of the needed observations. However, the time problem can be solved in a number of ways. One of the most successful solutions is to bring in some of the participants' supervisors as trained observers. This strategy, which is often used in assessment centers, has the added benefit of involving supervisors in the learning process in a more central way. Contracting with third parties to do observations is another option. In either case, some training is often necessary to provide consistency across observers.

Intellectual Skills

The term *intellectual skills* refers to learning how to do a skill that is mental rather than physical. Intellectual skills permit the learner to carry out the procedures and processes of a discipline. Examples of intellectual skills are running a computer program, creating a business case, and drawing a line analysis. Intellectual skills require learners to solve problems or perform tasks using information they have already learned. Balancing a checkbook is an intellectual skill that employs the previously learned knowledge of addition and subtraction. However, knowing math does not sufficiently enable someone to balance a checkbook. The additional learning is an intellectual skill that requires carrying out a procedure. Gagné and Briggs (1979) describe five levels of intellectual skills, each with increasing complexity: discriminations, concrete concepts, defined concepts, rules, and problem solving (Figure 5-2).

Intellectual Skills	Defined as the ability to:	For example:
Discriminations	Differentiate two things along one or more physical dimension.	To distinguish the sound of a functioning motor from one that is malfunctioning.
Concrete Concepts	Determine that a concrete object is a member of a category.	To recognize a number of three-sided objects of differing colors and sizes as triangles.
Defined Concepts	Demonstrate the meaning of some class of objects, events, or relations.	To identify the department's internal customers.
Rules	Apply a concept in a number of different situations.	To use commas correctly in sentences.
Problem Solving	Use rules (often more than one) to invent solutions to problems that are new to the learner.	To find a way to motivate a specific employee.

Figure 5-2. Levels of Intellectual Skills

Intellectual skills are measured by having the learner demonstrate that he or she can perform the skill. As with motor skills, the demonstration can be judged by a checklist, by a rating scale, or by the product. If the intellectual skill is interviewing, a checklist might be constructed for a third party to complete while observing the learner in role playing. If the intellectual skill is determining the correct sample size for a given vendor lot, the final answer of the computation can be judged as the product. It is not possible to determine if an intellectual skill can be performed by asking the participant to do a nonperformance task such as stating the three types of questions that can be used in an interview or remembering the formula for computing sample size.

In some demonstrations of a skill it is possible to determine not only whether the skill has been performed correctly, but also to determine what understanding is lacking in unsuccessful demonstrations. For example, if an employee learning to write business letters does not start each new paragraph with a new thought, it is possible to conclude that he or she does not understand how to use paragraphing.

In other situations it is possible only to determine correctness; to ascertain what went wrong, it is necessary to measure the verbal information that supports the skill. For example, in an automated materials handling program, if the employee does not input the appropriate code, it is difficult to know if the employee did not know (a) the code, (b) how to enter the code, (c) that a code should be entered, and so on. For both motor and intellectual skills it is sometimes necessary to measure the verbal information that supports the skill in order to decide how to remediate the learner or to improve the learning event.

In determining how to construct performance demonstrations of intellectual skills and motor skills, a major consideration is that the demonstration approximate, as closely as possible, how the learner will perform the skill on the job. For example, if the participant were demonstrating the skill of writing a critical incident, it would be a closer approximation of reality to have the participant view an incident being acted out than to ask him or her to react to a written description of the incident.

In judging intellectual skills during the learning event, trainers are often faced with the same time constraints they face with motor skills. Again, involving others in the evaluation is a viable solution. If accomplishing the intellectual skill will take a lengthy period of time—for example, for participants to demonstrate that they can write a business case—the task can be assigned to be completed after the participant is back on the job.

Verbal Information

Verbal information refers to the facts and organized knowledge that the learner stores in memory. Examples of verbal information outcomes are the definition of the term "group technology," the principles of just-in-time manufacturing, and the formula for determining standard deviation. Verbal information is often referred to as knowing "that" something is, rather than knowing "how" to do something, which is an intellectual skill.

In measuring verbal information, no problem solving is required; participants simply are asked to recall information. The recall does not have to be total: asking for the gist of an article or paragraph still gauges verbal information. Verbal information is generally tested by objective measures such as multiple-choice, true/false, matching, short-answer, and fill-in-the-blank questions. Multiple-choice questions are considered optimal both for ease of grading and for reducing the possibility of guessing. Matching items are also easy to grade but are appropriate for a more limited type of information, such as definitions, dates, and problems/solutions. True/false questions also provide ease in grading; however, participants have a 50-percent chance of guessing the right answer, so a greater number of items must be constructed. Completion items are time-consuming to grade and therefore are most useful when the total number of measures to be scored is small.

It should be noted that it is also possible to use objective measures for some intellectual skills. In such cases, questions are formulated so as to require participants to perform the task in order to get the answer and then record the answer on the form. For example, if participants have gone through the process of computing an interest rate, they may then answer multiple-choice or fill-in-the-blank questions.

Attitudes

The term *attitude* refers to the internal states that influence the course of action a learner chooses. For example, a manager's attitude toward quality affects the choices he or she makes about shipping a product that has not been fully tested when pressured by end-of-quarter goals. Other examples of attitude include commitment to pushing decisions down in the organization, valuing the use of statistics in process control, and believing that just-in-time manufacturing is needed in the organization.

Changes in attitude are legitimate outcomes that instructors teach toward and expect from learning events. Attitudes can be evaluated through attitudinal rating scales such as semantic differentials. A major concern in using rating scales is that they represent what Argyris (1985) calls *espoused theories*, versus *theories-in-use*. Espoused theories are those that individuals say—both to themselves and to others—guide their actions. *Theories-in-use* are those that actually guide a person's actions. The individual often is not even consciously aware of his or her theories-in-use, and the two theories very often are incongruent. For example, managers could indicate and believe that they favor equal opportunity in hiring, yet not choose to hire females into managerial positions when the opportunity arises. Attitude scales are limited to the collecting information about espoused theories.

A more sophisticated way of evaluating attitude is to predict the behavior that would result if the attitude were internalized, and then to measure the frequency of that behavior or change in behavior. For example, if the concept of customer service is valued by employees, more interdepartmental meetings would be expected to occur as a result of efforts to identify internal customer needs.

None of the above techniques provides totally reliable measures of attitude change; yet these measures, as imperfect as they are, provide useful information. By utilizing measures of attitude before and after the learning event, evaluators can determine the extent to which the event has affected the attitudes of participants.

One of the ways that learning events attempt to influence attitude is by providing verbal information that supports the need for a new way of functioning. Under such circumstances, it is possible to evaluate verbal information as an indirect measure of attitude. For example, if the intent is to influence participants to wear seat belts, quoting information on the number of lives saved per year by seat belts may change attitudes. If participants can recall that figure on an objective measure, they have learned the information that supports the attitude.

Cognitive Strategies

Cognitive strategies are a subset of intellectual skills that govern the individual's behavior in learning, remembering, and thinking. They are a kind of control strategy for learning that is not related to a specific discipline; unlike other intellectual skills, they apply across disciplines. Examples of cognitive strategies are problem reframing, critical reflection, and creative thinking.

As new and more creative solutions have become increasingly valued in organizations, learning events with cognitive strategies as the outcome have proliferated. Learning events that deal with cognitive strategies may teach how to break a problem up into parts; how to work backwards from a goal; how to seek inconsistencies in an argument; or how to use analogies in thinking.

The evaluation of cognitive strategies is accomplished through performance demonstration. It differs, however, from the evaluation of other intellectual skills in that standards cannot be established for the product or performance, because what is wanted is something novel. Of the five outcomes of instruction, least is known about how to learn and how to evaluate cognitive strategies.

Each of the five outcomes has been discussed as though a typical learning event deals with one outcome exclusively. Clearly, this is not so. Most learning involves more than one outcome, such as in the case of a materials management program in which trainers measure both the intellectual skill of coding materials correctly and the verbal information of the names of the codes themselves. Evaluation of a learning event often requires several tools, such as a demonstration of an intellectual skill using a checklist, a semantic differential to measure attitude, and multiple-choice items to measure verbal knowledge. To review the initial premise of this chapter, two considerations must govern the selection of appropriate measurement tools:

1. Measures should match the type of learning outcome intended for the learning event; and

2. Measures should approximate, as closely as possible, how the skill, knowledge, or attitude will be used on the job.

Problems Related to Introducing Performance Measures [1]

Introduction of performance measures into an organization that previously has used only participant reaction forms has the potential to improve significantly the effectiveness of HRD. However, evaluation carries with it a new set of problems for HRD to address. Four groups of stakeholders express concerns about evaluation: instructors, participants, HRD managers, and line managers. In this chapter the concerns of each group are delineated and possible solutions are suggested. Although some of the problems cannot be avoided, in many cases they can be lessened by anticipating their occurrence and by addressing them in advance with the stakeholders.

INSTRUCTOR CONCERNS

Instructors express the following three concerns about implementing performance measures:

1. Concerns about being judged;

2. Concerns about time lost from teaching; and

3. Concerns about the treatment of students as adults.

---

[1]The author gratefully acknowledges the assistance of Frank Kelly in the preparation of this chapter.

Instructor Concerns About Being Judged

In most organizations, instructor competence is judged by the ratings each instructor receives on participant reaction forms administered at the end of a learning event, and the number of participants that the learning event can attract (see Chapter 3). When performance measures are introduced, instructors often are concerned that participants will dislike being evaluated and will counter by giving the instructor poor ratings on the participant reaction forms. Likewise, instructors are concerned that potential participants will learn that performance measures are in use and will therefore not voluntarily participate in learning events.

Both of these instructor concerns occur in initiating evaluation in an organization in which evaluation has not been the norm. Thus, it would be expected that such concerns would abate as evaluation became an accepted practice in the organization. However, because it is often instructors on whom the extra burden of evaluation falls, it is critical to deal with their concerns initially.

The most fruitful way to deal with these issues is to meet with the instructors as a group, allowing them to voice their concerns and to jointly arrive at a solution. Solutions that have worked in some organizations include:

- Eliminating the participant reaction forms;
- Modifying the forms so that comparisons cannot be made (changing the scale or questions); and
- Conducting a pilot study to determine if performance measures do lower ratings or reduce numbers.

A second concern instructors express is that HRD management might use the results of the participant measures of learning to judge the instructors. Instructors recognize that despite their skill as instructors, they have only limited control over how much participants learn. Other factors, such as the participants' prerequisite skills, participants' level of interest, and the amount of time participants are absent from the learning event, all play significant roles in the results. Thus, some discussion about accountability is needed.

Time Lost from Teaching

Instructors generally feel that the time allotted for any learning event is too short to cover all of the necessary material. The prospect of designating several hours for measurement causes instructors great distress. However, when instructors use premeasures to determine what participants already know, they invariably discover portions of the material that they do not need to cover or on which they can spend less time.

A second important consideration is that participants actually retain what they have learned longer if they have an opportunity to demonstrate their skill or knowledge near the end of the learning event. Thus, instead of taking time away from learning, the use of performance measures is actually a very effective learning activity for participants. This fact can be demonstrated easily in any learning event that occurs a number of times. As a pilot study, administer performance measures in half the sessions and no performance measures in the other sessions. Six weeks later, administer the performance measures again to determine which groups have retained the most.

Much of the time-consuming activity in performance measures is in scoring and in observing functions, which can be done by personnel other than instructors. By providing assistance for these functions some of the time taken away from teaching can be reduced.

Treatment of Students as Adults

Instructors express concern that requiring participants to demonstrate their learning will cause them to feel like schoolchildren. Many instructors consider themselves to have an unspoken contract with participants: as adults, participants have the right to get as much or as little out of a learning event as they choose. The essence of this issue is whether participants should be held accountable for learning.

Some instructors try to avoid the issue by making a joke of the measure. However, that tactic becomes self-defeating, because unless participants make an honest effort to demonstrate their knowledge, the measure has little or no meaning. Others try to deal with the discomfort by telling participants that the measure is only to improve the course, not to judge them. If, indeed, the information will not be made available through a database or as feedback to their supervisors, that rationale can be used. However, in many cases the data are recorded and are fed back, so that rationale cannot be used.

The most beneficial solution may be to provide the instructor with a protocol to follow in administering the performance measure. Guidelines for establishing a protocol are outlined in Chapter 19. The protocol provides words for the instructor to use in explaining why the performance measures are being administered, and it explains the need for measures in terms of quality or in terms of the importance of the skill. In some situations instructors have worked together to arrive at an appropriate protocol for introducing the performance measure.

PARTICIPANT CONCERNS

Participants also experience concerns when evaluation is introduced. However, in many cases the participants' concerns are minimal and tend to be exaggerated by other stakeholders. For example, in one organization instructors worried about asking participants to put their names on the performance measure that was administered. In order to score and to return the forms, as well as to relate the data to the premeasure, instructors needed some identification on each paper. Several schemes were invented, the most elaborate of which was to ask participants to label their papers as follows: "Write the first initial of your mother's maiden name, the last two numbers of your social security number, and your middle initial." Other instructors asked participants to write in a nickname or draw in a symbol. These schemes created an unbelievable confusion of papers. Participants could not remember the symbols or the sequence they had invented. Finally in desperation, an instructor in one course simply asked participants to write their names on the top of the forms. The participants did so and no one complained. The instructor tried it again in the next course; surprisingly, no one there complained either. Eventually, all of the instructors took the easy route. After more than two thousand performance measures, no concerns surfaced. The fear of using names turned out to be an misconception on the part of the instructors. Participants do, however, have the following valid concerns:

- Encountering a performance measure unexpectedly;
- Anxieties about learning problems; and
- Questions about who will see the results.

Encountering a Performance Measure Unexpectedly

Because evaluation measures were used infrequently in most organizations in the past, participants do not expect that they will need to demonstrate that they have learned. They may even see participation in a learning event as a way to avoid the stress of work for a time. Participants who are unexpectedly faced with having to prove that they have learned can feel deceived.

This problem can be handled by making sure that participants know *before they decide to participate* that an evaluation measure will be administered. It may be appropriate to include this information in the course description in the catalog or announcement. Advance information not only reduces the surprise, but also allows participants to adjust their own attitudes about the seriousness of attending a learning event.

Anxieties About Learning Problems

Certain learning problems may cause anxiety in a small percentage of participants, such as the following:

- Participants who do not possess a sufficient reading level to read the materials or performance measures;
- Participants who do not speak or understand English well enough to comprehend the content or the performance measures;
- Participants who experience test anxiety; or
- Participants who have learning disabilities.

It is difficult to deal openly with any of these issues because many people are extraordinarily sensitive about them. To be most helpful, an instructor can say, "If anyone has problems with the performance measure because of language or some disability, please see me during a break so that we can make whatever arrangements are necessary for you to be successful." Situations then can be dealt with on a one-to-one basis. When reading is a problem, offering to judge the participant's understanding by holding a discussion or reading the directions to him or her can be helpful. Obviously, attempting to steer the participant toward literacy courses also would be useful. In the case of poor skills in English, allowing the participant to bring a translator may be useful. Individuals with learning disabilities often simply need extra time. Multiple-choice questions are sometimes easier for the learning disabled than fill-in-the-blank or short-answer questions. Again, offering to substitute a discussion or to have someone read the performance measure to the person is often a workable solution. Learning-disabled adults can have a variety of disabilities, including reading, writing, spelling, and math, any of which could cause a problem in demonstrating performance. Test anxiety can be dealt with by making the situation as nonthreatening as possible, perhaps at the participant's work site or in a comfortable setting.

Questions About Who Will See the Results

Participants can be concerned about who will see the results of their performance demonstrations. However, the concern is lessened considerably if performance measures are validated, competencies are directly related to their jobs, and participants have been informed in advance that the measures will be administered. Specific criteria that should be met before performance data are made available to others are discussed in Chapter 12.

HRD MANAGER CONCERNS

Human resource development managers express the following three concerns about implementing evaluation:

- Costs of evaluation;
- Consequences of negative results; and
- Evaluating will open a Pandora's box.

Costs of Evaluation

The costs associated with the evaluation of training take many forms. The most significant cost is personnel, which constitutes about 75 percent of the total amount spent on evaluation. The time involvement is in four areas: interaction with HRD's customers, constructing and validating measurement tools, administering the evaluation, and implementing decisions based on the results.

Increased interaction with the customer is time consuming both for HRD and for management. This concern is presented in detail in Chapter 2.

Designing valid performance measurements tools also represents a cost. If such expertise does not exist within the organization, it must be developed or purchased. Even given expertise, the process of designing and validating measurement tools is lengthy. Tools are developed, tested, revised, retested, and so on. Performance tools may go through four or five iterations before they can be considered valid and reliable. This is true of objective measures, performance demonstrations, checklists, surveys, and other tools. The components associated with performance measures also need to be developed, such as scoring keys, protocols for administration, and formats for databases.

Costs involved in administering the performance measurement differ according to the type of tool that is used. Requirements might include observers, scorers, data entry personnel, photocopying, additional equipment, and so on. Additional costs are associated with summarizing and constructing reports of the data. In some instances, statistical processes are applied, with the accompanying costs of personnel and computer time.

Finally, implementation of the decisions may have associated costs, such as in the case of a learning event that needs to be substantially revised to produce an acceptable level of learning.

The total cost for evaluation is usually estimated to be about 9 percent of the cost of a training event. Some of the costs are one-time costs, such as the development of the tools; other costs are incurred each time the evaluation is administered, such as scoring and data entry. Costs are higher if the organization has little experience with evaluation and lower as experience is gained. Factors that influence the level of costs are illustrated in Figure 6-1.

The cost of evaluation raises the issue of whether it is cost effective to evaluate all learning events, given that the organization may have a lengthy roster of courses that are taught on a regular basis. Clearly, evaluation is more cost effective if it is a part of the initial design effort. Therefore, first priority for evaluation dollars might be given to learning events that are under development. However, most organizations include many courses in their curriculum that do not currently have an evaluation component and for which funds would have to be allocated to construct such a component. If all existing courses cannot be evaluated because of cost, criteria for selecting which courses to give evaluation priority might include the following:

- The length of time the course is expected to be viable;
- The importance of the course in meeting the organization's goals;
- The size of the target audience; and
- The amount of course revision that would be required to construct evaluation measures.

Variable	Increasing Cost →				
Previous evaluation experience of the HRD staff	Low 1	2	3	4	High 5
Number of purposes for the evaluation	Low 1	2	3	4	High 5
Length of organization's experience with HRD evaluation	Short 1	2	3	4	Long 5
Number of data items to be completed, scored, and analyzed	Few 1	2	3	4	Many 5
Number of participants involved	Few 1	2	3	4	Many 5
Size/complexity of organization	Small/Simple 1	2	3	Large/Complex 4	5
Number of stakeholders/customers	Few 1	2	3	4	Many 5
Degree of automation of scoring and data input	High 1	2	3	4	Low 5

Figure 6-1. Variables in Estimating Costs of Evaluation

Consequences of Negative Results

Evaluation data could show that not much learning occurred during the learning event. In fact, if the major emphasis in HRD in past years has been on attracting participants to the courses, fear of negative results may well be a valid fear, for the reasons discussed in Chapter 3. Human resource development professionals face the reality that if evaluation data are available, line management could request to see them. Anticipating that the data may be unfavorable, HRD managers might have serious concerns about even beginning an evaluation process.

In one organization, a statistics course for manufacturing personnel had been taught for over two years. Calculating only salary for the one thousand participants who were enrolled over that period, the cost was close to $720,000. The typical participant-reaction forms were consistently very positive in terms of content, relevance, and instructor. When performance measures were introduced, however, it became clear that participants were able to demonstrate performance only on the concepts that were taught early in the course—about 25 percent of the content covered. As a result of the evaluation, the content was divided into three courses; less material was covered in a single course, and time was made available for additional practice. The concern of HRD management in this case was who might see the data before the problem could be corrected.

No simple solutions exist for this concern. In some organizations, HRD negotiates a period of time in which to get its house in order before publishing data. The most viable process may be to move slowly enough to correct the problems that the evaluation reveals, so that data from both before and after the correction are available.

Evaluating Will Open Pandora's Box

As illustrated in the preceding example, evaluation points out problems that HRD then must address. For instance, evaluation can reveal the following:

- Inadequate needs assessment has been done;
- The process of selecting participants results in employees' sitting through courses that have little relevance to them;
- Course descriptions are inaccurate; and/or
- Courses need substantial revision to result in learning.

For HRD managers, evaluation is a double-edged sword. On the one hand it reveals a myriad of problems that then must be corrected; on the other hand, evaluation is the only way to get the data needed to increase HRD's effectiveness.

LINE MANAGEMENT CONCERNS

Line management has the following five concerns:

- Evaluation could lengthen the time employees are away from their jobs;
- Holding to performance criteria could delay employees' being certified;
- Usage data could reveal poor management practices;
- Additional responsibility could be expected; and
- Time would be taken from work to collect usage data.

The last three concerns pertain more to measures of on-the-job usage and will be discussed in Chapter 8. The first two will be discussed in this section.

Time Away From Jobs

Line management expresses concern that adding performance measures to learning events would lengthen the amount of time employees have to spend away from work. As discussed previously, adding performance measures typically does not result in longer learning events; rather, it is more usual for evaluation to reveal parts of the content that can be eliminated.

Like instructors, managers often do not realize that a performance measure can actually increase learning and retention. As suggested in the instructor section, conducting a pilot study to illustrate the increased learning resulting from the use of performance measures can provide convincing evidence that the measures are beneficial.

Delay in Certification

A second concern applies to situations involving certification, either through the organization's own policies or via external regulations. In one organization, field service representatives attended training periodically to learn the installation and repair for new equipment on the market. Instructors in the course experienced considerable pressure from field service management to certify the representatives so that they would be ready.

One possible solution to this concern is to guarantee the learning; that is, if the participant does not meet the minimum criteria established, the instructor continues to work with the employee until the criteria are met. This solution requires that instructors build more flexibility into their schedules.

Line management's concerns are most pressing in the absence of dialog between line management and HRD. As line management participates in all phases of the HRD quality process, the concerns lessen.

Measuring the Design and Delivery of a Learning Event

Evaluation for the purpose of improving the learning event has been discussed in terms of measuring participants' learning. Evaluation also needs to be discussed in terms of the following two factors:

- The design and delivery of the learning event, and
- The analysis of the participant profile.

This chapter addresses design and delivery and asks the following three questions related to quality:

- Does the design contain the elements of good instruction?
- Was the intent of the design carried out in the classroom?
- Did the instructor use appropriate techniques of instruction?

ELEMENTS OF GOOD INSTRUCTION

Does the design contain the elements of good instruction? An effective process for answering this question is to review the course materials using a predetermined checklist or rating scale. A review panel, composed of the various stakeholders in the instructional process, examines each new course. This review can occur before the course is taught the first time or after the first performance data are available. In some organizations, instructors themselves serve as the review team; in others, external reviewers who have expertise in design are used in this capacity. The review team examines the course objectives, participant materials, instructor's guide, and media, serving as a quality check for one part of the HRD process.

A number of excellent texts and articles can provide guidance in selecting the factors to include in the checklist or rating scale. However, no generic list of factors is appropriate for all organizations; each organization needs to construct its own tool for this purpose. Four steps are involved in the process. First, the best thinking of the experts is reviewed and formatted into items for the tool. Second, the experts' items are discussed and modified by the stakeholders (the instructors, designers, customers, and HRD management) within that specific organization. Third, the tool is field tested and revised. Fourth, the tool is employed with considerable discretion, that is, treated as a set of guidelines, rather than as criteria.

CARRYING OUT THE DESIGN
IN THE CLASSROOM

Was the intent of the design carried out in the classroom? The only way to determine if the design has been actually carried out is to observe the instruction, either in person or by videotape. The reviewer can be an external observer with expertise in course design, another instructor, the HRD manager, or a person with similar qualifications. The reviewer receives the course outline with expected times noted, the instructor's manual, and the participants' materials. His or her task is to observe how closely the actual instruction followed what was planned in terms of the sequence of activities, time allocations for activities, and activities that were excluded or added.

This evaluation is a time-consuming one, and probably does not need to take place unless the results of the performance data are poor. However, it is a critical step under those circumstances.

The original design itself should not be altered to compensate for poor results if the design were not fully implemented.

APPROPRIATE TECHNIQUES OF INSTRUCTION

Did the instructor use appropriate techniques of instruction? The final evaluation form is the most controversial, both in terms of what constitutes good teaching and in terms of who does the observing. Therefore, instructor discussion and agreement as to the elements to be measured is critical. The four steps provided for constructing the design form apply to constructing the instructional checklist or rating scale as well:

1. Utilize the advice of experts as a starting point in designing the items for the checklist or rating scale.
2. Modify the items on the basis of stakeholder input and reach consensus on the final draft;
3. Field test the tool and revise it as needed; and
4. Employ the tool with discretion.

The fourth step is particularly important. First, little agreement exists among teaching professionals about what constitutes effective instructor behavior. The controversies are not unlike the issues concerning leadership; to some degree effectiveness in both appears to be idiosyncratic. Therefore, the checklist or rating scale, regardless of how well constructed, can serve only as a guide.

Second, each of Gagné's learning outcomes requires the instructor to function in a different manner. Some of the differences can be built into the design, but many rely on the skill of the instructor. Any form that evaluates instruction must be adjusted for each specific learning outcome.

The purpose of the checklist or rating scale is to collect information to improve the delivery of the learning event. Once created and accepted by instructors, it can also serve as a tool for performance evaluation of the instructors. This then becomes the fairest way of evaluating instructors—certainly more fair than the results of participant reaction forms or participant scores on performance measures.

A form is provided in Figure 7-1 as a starting point for organizations to construct their own tools. Both design and instructional elements are represented in this sample form; instructional elements appear in lower-case letters and design elements appear in upper-case letters.

Any tool represents the knowledge and bias of those who constructed it; that is true of this tool as well. Although the tool is based on learning theory and instructional design principles, ultimately both the choice of items and the wording represents the author's biases about what constitutes good instruction.

An explanation of several items is embedded in the questionnaire. A copy of the questionnaire without the explanatory comments is found in Appendix A.

The tools discussed in this chapter are appropriate for situations in which the learning has been specified in advance and the course has been designed to that end. As organizations are changing, however, they find a need for different kinds of learning that would be evaluated in different ways.

Increasingly, organizations are less likely to know in advance the answers they need. Much of the critical information needed in organizations has to be invented in the process of responding to changing forces. To deal with change and with increased competition, organizations are empowering their employees and seeking greater participation from them. Employees are being asked to reflect continually on their own actions to discover more effective ways of functioning within the organization—to find new problems as well as to create new and innovative solutions for current problems.

Under such circumstances, courses that provide expert or known answers are only one of the forms of learning required. Other forms of learning, in which the content is not structured but grows out of the work situation, are increasingly important. Learning processes are needed that encourage employees to reflect on and learn from ongoing experience and to challenge the taken-for-granted assumptions of the organization.

In this new type of learning situation, what is to be learned cannot be specified in advance, but in fact grows out of the participants' critical thinking. The instructor is a facilitator of the learning rather than a teacher who has answers. The facilitator assists with process, but even then does not bear sole responsibility; instead, he or she offers suggestions for the group to consider.

A very different kind of checklist is needed to evaluate the facilitator in this learning environment, similar to that depicted in Figure 7-2 (page 88). Again, an organization would need to modify the checklist for its own use.

**INSTRUCTOR BEHAVIORS AND COURSE DESIGN
OBSERVATION FORM**

Course Name_____ #_____ Module #_____

Organization_____ Location _____

Instructor_____ Length of course _____

Evaluator_____ Date reviewed _____

Instructions: Some items ask you to consider the actions of the instructor over the entire observation period; those items are scaled. For other items, only a check mark is needed if the action occurred. If you did not have an opportunity to observe the action, place a check in the "No opportunity to observe" blank. The comments line is the most important response; please use it freely.

I. INTRODUCTION

	No opportunity to observe	*Yes*
A. Introduced self	_____	_____

(Did the instructor establish experiential or academic credibility? What tone was established?)

Comments_____

**Figure 7-1. Instructor Behaviors and Course Design—
Observation Form**

B. Introduced participants

	No opportunity to observe	Yes
1. Expressed interest in participants	_____	_____

(To what extent did the instructor comment on or ask further questions of participants to indicate that their experiences and positions were important?)

Comments_____

	Authority		Collaborator	
2. Established self as:	1 2	3	4	5

(Indicate the nature of the relationship that the instructor established with the participants. Different instructors may function best at different points on the scale.)

Comments_____

C. Introduction of the course

	No opportunity to observe	Yes
1. Communicated agenda/logistics	_____	_____

Comments_____

	No opportunity to observe	Yes
2. PROVIDED COURSE OVERVIEW	_____	_____

Comments_____

	No opportunity to observe	Yes
3. COMMUNICATED COURSE OBJECTIVES	_____	_____

Comments_____

	No opportunity to observe	Yes
4. MODULE OBJECTIVES ARE MEASURABLE	_____	_____

Comments_____

Figure 7-1 (continued). Instructor Behaviors and Course Design— Observation Form

	Rarely			Consistently	
5. COMMUNICATED MODULE OBJECTIVES	1	2	3	4	5

Comments_____

Instructions: Sections II through VII each apply to a different method of instruction. Each is marked only if that type of instruction was employed.

II. LECTURE

A. Teaching technique

	Unorganized			Organized	
1. Presentation	1	2	3	4	5

Comments_____

	Rarely			Consistently	
2. Reminded participants of related knowledge	1	2	3	4	5

(For verbal information, it is helpful for participants to recall related knowledge so that they have memory hooks for the new information.)

Comments_____

	Rarely			Consistently	
3. Used variety of examples for concepts	1	2	3	4	5

(For Intellectual skills, using a variety of examples helps to differentiate concepts and assists in transfer.)

Comments_____

B. Style

	Unacceptable			Acceptable	
1. Style of presentation for this audience	1	2	3	4	5

Comments_____

	Rarely			Consistently	
2. Sought feedback on participant understanding	1	2	3	4	5

**Figure 7-1 (continued). Instructor Behaviors and Course Design—
Observation Form**

(The instructor asks questions to check how well participants are understanding what is being said, so that he/she can alter the speed, provide additional examples, and so on.)

Comments_____

	Too slow			*Too fast*	
3. Pacing appropriate for the density	1	2	3	4	5

(This question refers to the complexity of the material presented. For extremely complex or dense content, the learner needs a considerable amount of pausing and thinking time interspersed with the lecture.)

Comments_____

	Easily got off topic			*Stayed focused*	
4. Stayed on topic	1	2	3	4	5

Comments_____

C. Knowledge of subject matter

	Little knowledge			*Extensive knowledge*	
1. Instructor answers displayed:	1	2	3	4	5

Comments_____

	Uncertain			*Confident*	
2. Related to material, instructor appeared:	1	2	3	4	5

Comments_____

III. LEADING A DISCUSSION

	Rarely			*Consistently*	
A. Asked open-ended questions	1	2	3	4	5

(Closed questions are appropriate to determine if participants are grasping the concepts the instructor is teaching. Open-ended questions invite critical thinking about the concepts.)

Comments_____

Figure 7-1 (continued). Instructor Behaviors and Course Design— Observation Form

	Rarely			*Consistently*	
B. Refrained from responding to all comments	1	2	3	4	5

(This discussion technique moves the focus away from the leader. By refraining from commenting on each participant's statements, the instructor centers the discussion among the participants.)

Comments_____

	Rarely			*Consistently*	
C. Prevented a few from dominating	1	2	3	4	5

Comments_____

	Rarely			*Consistently*	
D. Kept discussion on topic	1	2	3	4	5

Comments_____

IV. EXPERIENTIAL ACTIVITIES

	No opportunity to observe	*Yes*
A. Stated purpose/outcome of activity	_____	_____

(Instructors sometimes do not spend sufficient time explaining the purpose of an activity, leaving participants to wonder what they are expected to get out of it. An evaluation item related to "purpose" appears at the beginning of each section.)

Comments_____

	Confusing			*Clear*	
B. Instructions were:	1	2	3	4	5

Comments_____

C. Debriefed activity

	No opportunity to observe	*Yes*
1. Discussed feelings and reactions	_____	_____

Figure 7-1 (continued). Instructor Behaviors and Course Design— Observation Form

(Many experiential activities result in affective as well as cognitive learning. If activities are not thoroughly debriefed on both levels, participants can leave with unresolved issues.)

Comments_____

	No opportunity to observe	*Yes*
2. Sought patterns in the data	_____	_____

(Items 2 and 3 are paired items. Often at the end of experiential activities, data are collected. Item 2 refers to the analysis of that data, and item 3 to the conclusions that can be drawn from it. In the interest of time, these important steps of experiential activities are often slighted.)

Comments_____

	No opportunity to observe	*Yes*
3. Helped group reach generalizations	_____	_____

Comments_____

	No opportunity to observe	*Yes*
4. Helped group explore ways to apply findings	_____	_____

Comments_____

V. SKILL PRACTICE

A. Management of the skill practice

	No opportunity to observe	*Yes*
1. Stated purpose of the skill practice	_____	_____

Comments_____

	Confusing			*Clear*
2. Instructions were:	1 2	3	4	5

Comments_____

**Figure 7-1 (continued). Instructor Behaviors and Course Design—
Observation Form**

	No opportunity to observe	Yes
3. Provided instructions for peer feedback	_____	_____

(The quality of participants' feedback to each other is considerably improved if the instructor provides guidelines and demonstrates how to give feedback.)

Comments_____

	No opportunity to observe	Yes
4. Instructor offered appropriate feedback	_____	_____

Comments_____

	No opportunity to observe	Yes
5. Debriefed practice	_____	_____

Comments_____

B. Time for practice

	No opportunity to observe	Yes
1. ADEQUATE PRACTICE TIME WAS ALLOCATED	_____	_____

Comments_____

	No opportunity to observe	Yes
2. ADEQUATE NUMBER OF SKILL PRACTICES WERE PROVIDED	_____	_____

Comments_____

VI. INSTRUMENTATION

	Confusing			Clear	
A. Instructions were:	1	2	3	4	5

Comments_____

**Figure 7-1 (continued). Instructor Behaviors and Course Design—
Observation Form**

	No opportunity to observe	Yes
B. Explained theory of instrument	_____	_____

(In order for participants to make their own decisions about the value of an instrument, some knowledge of the theory from which it is derived is necessary.)

Comments_____

	Confusing			Clear	
C. Directions for scoring:	1	2	3	4	5

Comments_____

	No opportunity to observe	Yes
D. Provided adequate interpretation	_____	_____

Comments_____

	No opportunity to observe	Yes
E. Processed the experience	_____	_____

Comments_____

	No opportunity to observe	Yes
F. Avoided defending instrument	_____	_____

(Instructors are sometimes inclined to defend an instrument or its results rather than allowing participants to determine the value for themselves.)

Comments_____

VII. CLASSROOM MANAGEMENT

A. Difficult participants

	Discourteous			Courteous	
1. Handled angry participants with courtesy	1	2	3	4	5

Comments_____

**Figure 7-1 (continued). Instructor Behaviors and Course Design—
Observation Form**

	Defended position			Open to others
2. Allowed for differing views	1	2	3	4	5

(This item refers to the extent to which the instructor is open to being influenced by the participants' ideas and opinions.)

Comments_____

	Rarely			Consistently
3. Prevented domination by a few participants	1	2	3	4	5

Comments_____

	Rarely			Consistently
4. Controlled outside conversations	1	2	3	4	5

Comments_____

B. Time

	No opportunity to observe	Yes
1. Began on time	_____	_____

Comments_____

	No opportunity to observe	Yes
2. Started on time after breaks	_____	_____

Comments_____

	No opportunity to observe	Yes
3. Ended on time	_____	_____

Comments_____

**Figure 7-1 (continued). Instructor Behaviors and Course Design—
Observation Form**

C. Room arrangement

	No opportunity to observe	Yes
1. Arrangement suited to type of instruction	_____	_____

Comments_____

	No opportunity to observe	Yes
2. Size of room appropriate	_____	_____

Comments_____

VIII. MEDIA

A. Introduction

	No opportunity to observe	Yes
1. Explained objective of media	_____	_____

Comments_____

	No opportunity to observe	Yes
2. Suggested what to watch for	_____	_____

Comments_____

B. Quality

	Unprofessional/Professional				
1. PROFESSIONAL QUALITY	1	2	3	4	5

Comments_____

	No opportunity to observe	Yes
2. CURRENT KNOWLEDGE	_____	_____

Comments_____

**Figure 7-1 (continued). Instructor Behaviors and Course Design—
Observation Form**

	No opportunity to observe	Yes
3. SATISFIES EEO REGULATIONS	_____	_____

Comments_____

	No opportunity to observe	Yes
C. Debriefed media	_____	_____

Comments_____

IX. CONCLUSION OF COURSE

	No opportunity to observe	Yes
A. Instructor summarized what had been taught	_____	_____

Comments_____

	No opportunity to observe	Yes
B. PARTICIPANTS CONSTRUCTED AN ACTION PLAN	_____	_____

Comments_____

	No opportunity to observe	Yes
C. Follow-up was established	_____	_____

Comments_____

X. EVALUATION

	No opportunity to observe	Yes
A. POSTTEST APPROPRIATE FOR OUTCOMES	_____	_____

Comments_____

Figure 7-1 (continued). Instructor Behaviors and Course Design— Observation Form

	No opportunity to observe	Yes
B. POSTTEST EVALUATED STATED OBJECTIVES	_____	_____

Comments_____

	No opportunity to observe	Yes
C. All objectives covered in the course	_____	_____

Comments_____

XI. PARTICIPANT MATERIALS

	No opportunity to observe	Yes
A. ADEQUATE GLOSSARY	_____	_____

Comments_____

	No opportunity to observe	Yes
B. ADEQUATE BIBLIOGRAPHY	_____	_____

Comments_____

	No opportunity to observe	Yes
C. NECESSARY PERFORMANCE AIDS PROVIDED	_____	_____

Comments_____

	Difficult to locate			Easy to locate	
D. ORGANIZED FOR EASE IN LOCATING ITEMS	1	2	3	4	5

Comments_____

**Figure 7-1 (continued). Instructor Behaviors and Course Design—
Observation Form**

	No opportunity to observe	Yes
E. APPROPRIATE READING LEVEL	_____	_____

Comments_____

XII. INSTRUCTOR MATERIALS

	Yes	No
Instructor's materials contain:		
1. Description of target population	_____	_____
2. Participant prerequisites	_____	_____
3. Recommended minimum and maximum numbers of participants	_____	_____
4. Suggested instructor qualifications	_____	_____
5. Recommended length of learning event	_____	_____
6. Recommended spacing and timing of modules	_____	_____
7. Facilities requirements	_____	_____
8. Equipment needs	_____	_____
9. List of participant materials	_____	_____
10. List of instructor materials	_____	_____
11. Evaluation design		
Suggested protocol	_____	_____
Instruments for end of learning event	_____	_____
Instruments for measuring on-the-job behaviors	_____	_____
Evidence of validation of instruments/norms	_____	_____
Scoring keys/suggested answers	_____	_____
Minimum criteria suggested	_____	_____
12. Supporting readings	_____	_____
13. References for further reading	_____	_____

**Figure 7-1 (continued). Instructor Behaviors and Course Design—
Observation Form**

CHECKLIST FOR FACILITATOR SKILLS

The Facilitator:

☐ Establishes a climate of openness, cooperation, and healthy confrontation.

☐ Designs opportunities for participants to learn from the perspectives, mistakes, and successes of others.

☐ Asks questions that assist participants in exploring the reasons behind their assumptions.

☐ Recognizes and confronts group assumptions.

☐ Facilitates group problem-solving strategies.

☐ Formulates questions that cause participants to feel challenged rather than criticized.

☐ Rejects the temptation to display his or her own knowledge and understanding.

☐ Acknowledges his or her own doubts and anxieties.

☐ Alters his or her opinions as a result of compelling arguments of participants.

☐ Stays involved in what is going on while observing own and others' behaviors.

☐ Effectively deals with emotions that participants aim at the facilitator.

☐ Encourages criticism (of the facilitator).

☐ Publicly acknowledges own errors, treating them as experiences from which to learn.

Figure 7-2. Checklist for Facilitator Skills

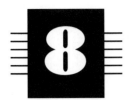

Increasing the Usage of Learning on the Job

Measures of usage are administered sometime after the learning event to collect data related to the use of the skills, knowledge, and attitudes on the job. Figure 8-1 lists a wide range of methods that can be employed to collect the data.

Collecting usage data serves two major purposes: (1) finding ways to increase use, and (2) making decisions about learning in the organization. This chapter discusses finding ways to increase the use; Chapter 12 addresses making decisions about learning in the organization.

The first purpose is accomplished by seeking answers to three questions:

1. What kinds of on-the-job assistance can the instructor offer to participants that would increase their implementation of the skills, knowledge, and attitudes?

2. In what ways does the learning event itself need to be modified to assist participants in implementing the skills, knowledge, and attitudes?

3. What organizational constraints are making the implementation of the skills, knowledge, and attitudes difficult?

ON-THE-JOB ASSISTANCE IN IMPLEMENTATION

Instructors tend to think that if participants have mastered a skill during the learning event, they are adequately prepared to implement it on the job. This rationale supposes that, unless faced with

Observation of performance
   Simulated work task
      Checklists
      Rating scales
      Product quality assessments
         Trainer
         Peers
         Supervisor
         Assessors (assessment center)
      Projects
      Case study
Surveys/Questionnaires

Interviews
      Individual
      Group
      Telephone
      In person
Anecdotal records
      Supervisor
      Self
      Peers
      Subordinates
      Instructor
         Critical incident
         Logs
         Tallies
         Journals
         Action audit
Records
      Created records of work results
      Existing business indicators
      Existing performance data (absenteeism,
         performance appraisal)
      Existing documents (e.g., minutes,
         reports)

Figure 8-1. Measures of Usage

an uncooperative supervisor or a similar constraint, participants will be able simply to transfer what they learned in the classroom to the job setting. Consequently, training literature on transfer of training primarily has focused either on what the supervisor needs to do to be supportive or on how the instructor can motivate the participant to want to use the skills.

However, research on the transfer of training does not support the view that the training adequately prepares participants to transfer the skills to the work place. Transfer is more appropriately thought of as another stage of learning, separate and apart from the initial mastery of the skills, knowledge, and attitudes. The learning in the transfer stage involves the following activities on the part of participants:

1. Making an initial decision as to whether the skill is appropriate for use in their situations;

2. Identifying opportunities to use the skill;

3. Modifying the skill to fit specific work situations;

4. Attempting the skill the first time;

5. Assessing the effectiveness of the initial attempt;

6. Modifying the skill on the basis of the initial attempt; and

7. Making the decision to use or not use the skill a second time.

Transfer of learning is facilitated by the assistance of a coach. The more complex the skill, the more necessary the coaching function. An important outcome of this assistance is that participants are more likely to experience the initial success that encourages continued use. Data (Showers, 1982) indicate that if an initial attempt to use a new skill is unsuccessful, participants are much less likely to try again.

Unfortunately, unaided first attempts at using new skills often fail. One reason for this is that participants must do two very difficult tasks at the same time. They must use a skill that has not been practiced long enough to be automatic, therefore requiring conscious thought. At the same time, they must modify the skill to fit the somewhat different situation that exists on the job. Under such circumstances, the likelihood of success is low.

In an attempt to be reassuring, instructors sometimes indicate that participants are fully prepared and that implementation will be easy; this can exacerbate the problem. If participants experience failure or only partial success, they may take that as evidence that the skill is not useful in their situations and decide not to try again.

Even if the goal is accomplished, the implementation is likely to have been awkward and uncomfortable. If a more familiar skill exists in participants' repertoires, they are likely to revert to that rather than to experience the discomfort.

Data collection enables the instructor to learn the nature of the coaching that is needed to increase the usage of specific skills, knowledge, and attitudes. Showers (1982) suggests three elements that can improve implementation: providing companionship, giving technical feedback, and analyzing the application. Results of the data collection might reveal the kind of help that is needed, which might include the following:

- To modify the SKA for a specific situation;
- To work with the participant to plan the implementation;
- To serve as a support;
- To act as a sounding board;
- To respond in an emergency; and/or
- To pave the way in difficult political situations.

Traditionally HRD professionals have not assumed responsibility for—nor been expected to assist with—implementation of skills on the job. However, that function is changing in many organizations as instructors' jobs are redefined to be instructors/consultants. In some organizations, 50 percent of the HRD professionals' time is spent facilitating learning events and the other 50 percent is spent coaching participants in implementing the new skills or processes. This allows the HRD professionals to observe, first hand, how well the customer's needs are being met, and to identify additional needs.

The argument against using instructors in a coaching capacity is that it removes them from the classroom and, therefore, less training will occur. If the classroom/coaching ratio were 50/50 as suggested above, then 50 percent fewer classes would be taught. Georgenson (1982) estimates that only 10 percent of the dollars spent on training results in behavioral change on the job. Using these figures, if coaching increased implementation by even 30 percent, the organization still would come out ahead.

Coaching the transfer process can also be done by a supervisor who has sufficient expertise in the specific skill. If he or she is able to serve in this capacity, the instructor can work in partnership with the supervisor; this ensures that the supervisor understands the transfer process and that the instructor obtains feedback about how the teaching of the skills in the classroom might be improved.

MODIFICATIONS OF THE LEARNING EVENT

The second set of data collected to increase usage is information on how the learning event itself could be modified. The following questions address this issue:

- Do participants need additional knowledge? Different skills? More practice?

- Do participants need greater organizational understanding? More theoretical knowledge so that they can alter procedures?

- Do participants need more in-depth knowledge because they are charged with teaching others these same skills?

- Do participants need less procedural knowledge because they are going to delegate the tasks?

- Do participants need job aids? Technical manuals?

For example, the data collected in one organization after a learning event on conflict revealed that participants were successful in using the skills to deal with conflict between subordinates, but that the processes were less workable when the conflict was with peers. To resolve conflict with peers, participants needed additional understanding and an opportunity to practice the peer situation during the learning event.

Several instructional techniques increase the likelihood that the participants will be able to transfer the intellectual skills from the classroom to the job. Each needs to be examined in light of usage data.

The first technique is to practice the skill in a manner that resembles the on-the-job situation as closely as possible. This technique is referred to in the transfer literature as "identical elements." As discussed above, the more the skill must be modified for the on-the-job situation, the more problematic the transfer. An instructor who spends time in the work site is more familiar with on-the-job conditions and better able to simulate them in the classroom.

The second technique is to organize the information. Organizing facilitates transfer because it makes the facts more readily available when they are needed. If participants are having difficulty recalling the information needed to support the use of the skills, the instructor may need to revise the presentation or the participant materials to provide better organization. Alternatively, the instructor may need to incorporate exercises that assist each participant in placing a personal and unique structure on complex material.

The third technique is to teach the underlying principles that support the skills. This technique is referred to as *far transfer*, as opposed to *near transfer*. Near transfer indicates that the participant can replicate specific skills on the job but lacks the knowledge of underlying principles that would permit him or her to modify the skill to fit new situations. *Far transfer* implies that the principles have been learned; however, less emphasis may have been placed on learning to implement the skill in a specific situation, thereby lessening initial success. Time limitations in most learning events require that either near or far transfer be emphasized. One of the functions of collecting usage data is to determine if this emphasis has been correctly placed.

The fourth instructional technique is the use of examples. Transfer is facilitated by the use of many examples and by providing variety in the examples (Gagné, 1985). Collecting usage data provides an excellent opportunity to identify relevant examples that can be used in the learning event.

The fifth technique, which will be discussed at greater length in the chapter on skill retention, is overlearning. *Overlearning* is continued practice of a skill after it can be performed correctly; its purpose is to lengthen the time the skill is retained.

Finally, there is some indication that goal setting at the end of a learning event will increase transfer (Wexley & Baldwin, 1986). Informing participants of what has and has not worked for others can help them to establish realistic goals. Awareness of the problems others have encountered allows participants to include strategies to overcome these problems in their plans.

IDENTIFYING ORGANIZATIONAL CONSTRAINTS TO USAGE

The third type of data to collect in order to increase usage of the learning is information about constraints. *Constraints* are variables that inhibit participants from implementing what they have learned on the job. That is not to imply that a constraint is intentional; most are inadvertent or occur out of lack of awareness. The following list of constraints incorporates the ideas of a number of authors who have identified factors related to performance (Gilbert, 1978; Harmon, 1984; House, 1968; Peters & O'Conner, 1980):

- The tools or equipment employed in using the skill are unavailable or are in short supply;
- Information needed as input to the process is unavailable or difficult to access;
- The delay between learning and the first opportunity to implement is too long;
- Other tasks take precedence over the use of the new skills;
- Materials or supplies needed to implement the new skills are unavailable;

- Needed cooperation from others cannot be obtained;

- Some of the consequences of implementing the new skills are negative;

- The budget necessary has not been allocated;

- The use of the skills violates the participant's values;

- Peers express disapproval of the use of the skills; and

- The participant's manager is not supportive of the use of the skills.

Identifying such constraints helps increase usage in two ways. First, understanding the constraints that participants face in implementation allows the instructor to incorporate awareness of the constraints in the learning event. For example, if it is known that the skill cannot be used for six weeks, either the learning event can be delayed or the skills can be practiced to a sufficient level (overlearned) that they will survive that length of delay.

The second way such data can be helpful is that they allow the HRD professional to provide the information on constraints to stakeholders who are in a position to remove or to modify them. For example, if supervisors are learning teamwork skills to facilitate their working more cooperatively with other supervisors across departments, usage data may reveal that an organizational policy—such as rank-ordering supervisors for merit pay—acts to prevent teamwork from occurring. Making upper management aware of this conflict would allow managers to make changes in the system or in their expectations.

COLLECTING USAGE DATA

This section discusses techniques for collecting usage data on each of learning outcomes discussed in Chapter 5: intellectual skills, motor skills, verbal information, attitude, and cognitive strategies.

On-the-job Measures of Intellectual Skills

A decision tree for the selection of on-the-job measures is displayed in Figure 8-2. Nine questions make up the decision tree. Each will be discussed in turn.

1. Is there an existing business indicator that is directly tied to the skill? The least costly and most satisfactory measure of usage is to measure the change in an existing business indicator that is tied directly to the use of the skill. The term *business indicator* is used here to mean data that the organization collects as a measure of effectiveness, such as inventory turnover or increased sales. "Directly tied" indicates a cause-and-effect relationship between the business indicator and the skill. Such indicators are rare. Most business indicators measure the effect of a large number of variables, so changing any one of them may or may not result in a change in the indicator. However, when such a skill is directly tied to a business indicator, data are collected simply by noting the baseline data before the learning event and at several intervals following implementation.

2. Are there existing performance data tied directly to the skill? *Performance data* are measures that the organization maintains because they influence effectiveness, including such things as absenteeism or performance ratings. Again, the criterion for using performance data as measures of usage is that the data be directly tied to the skill. Measurement for usage purposes consists of tracking prelearning and postlearning figures.

3. Do records exist that could be examined to determine if skills are being implemented? Using data that already exist for some other purpose is a cost-effective way to measure usage. Therefore, the first three questions in the decision tree query the use of existing data. Existing records include such things as minutes from meetings, reports, memos, and so on. For example, reviewing minutes will demonstrate whether or not an agenda is being followed in meetings. In one organization, reviewing the sign-on that was

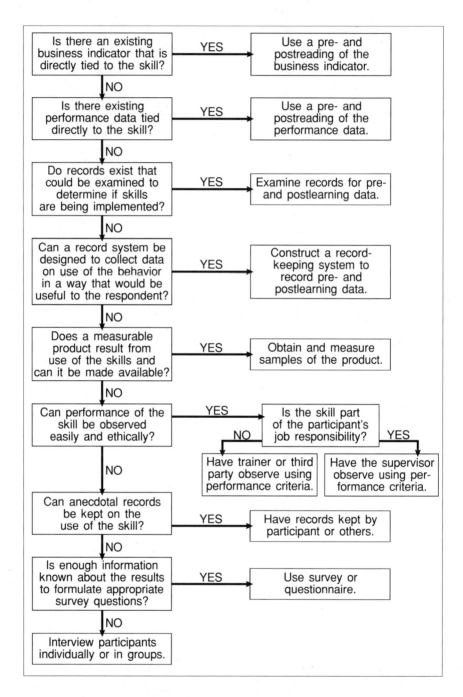

Figure 8-2. Decision Tree for Selecting Usage Measures

automatically recorded by the computer was used to determine how often a dedicated computer program had been utilized and by whom.

4. Can a record system be designed to collect data on the use of the behavior in a way that would be useful to the respondent? In some situations it is possible to construct a simple tally sheet or a checklist that someone (the participant, a supervisor, subordinates, or others) could use to collect data on the number of times a behavior occurs. This methodology is most useful if the record benefits the record keeper as well as the evaluator. Examples of such record systems would include a manager tallying the number of times he or she delegates, tracking the number of errors on forms, overhead charts that display scheduled versus actual production, and so on.

5. Does a measurable product result from use of the skills and can it be made available? In some situations, a product results from the use of the skills that can be evaluated against a checklist or rating scale. Such products might range from a computer program to a product design or a strategic plan. The task of the evaluator is to plan the collection of all or a sample of the products.

6. Can the performance of the skill be observed easily and ethically? There are two parts to this question. First, can the skill be observed? Under some circumstances, particularly in management development, intellectual skills are employed in situations that occur too sporadically to be easily observed by a third party. For example, the skill of empowering others is difficult to observe on a daily basis. Second, can the skill be observed ethically? Again, in certain situations, such as performance reviews, observation would be inappropriate. If the skill can be observed easily and ethically, then the next consideration is to determine who could observe it.

7. Is the skill a part of the participant's job responsibility? When the skill is part of the participant's job, his or her supervisor is the appropriate person to evaluate the skill. The HRD professional would provide the supervisor with validated checklists or rating scales and, if necessary, provide training in the use of the tools. If the skill is not a part of the participant's job, it may be more appropriate for the instructor or a third party to do the observation.

8. Can anecdotal records be kept on the use of the skill? Anecdotal records are used in situations in which the skill cannot be observed either because it occurs too sporadically or because it would be unethical. Records can be kept by the participant or the supervisor. There are a number of ways to keep such records, including critical incidents, journals, cases, or reports. If participants themselves are to keep the anecdotal records, specific directions need to be provided during the learning event itself. If supervisors are to record the anecdotes, training will be needed to ensure that usable data are reported.

9. Is enough information known about the results to formulate appropriate survey questions? When it is clear what questions should be asked or when it is important to obtain data from a large number of participants, surveys are helpful. However, many of the concerns discussed previously about participant reaction forms also apply to surveys. General questions such as "Were you able to put the learning to use on the job?" do not provide results that help to increase usage or to make decisions about the learning in the organization. Questions need to be pointed toward the specific intellectual skills involved, such as, "In the last three months, how many histograms have you constructed? Please state the title of each." It is often helpful to precede surveys by a series of interviews to formulate the questions.

10. Interview participants individually or in groups. Interviews are particularly valuable tools when the evaluator is seeking unanticipated information such as constraints to usage or novel ways the skill has been used. Interviews can be conducted with individuals either in person or by telephone. Group interviews can also be used to collect this kind of information. As in the case of observations, it may be possible to contract with external consultants to conduct interviews, perhaps at lower daily rate than trainer costs.

On-the-job Measures of Motor Skills

The measure of motor skills is similar whether the performance demonstration takes place during the learning event or as a post-learning-event measure; the major difference is who does the observation or product judging. During the learning event the observer is most likely to be the instructor or a designee. For the postmeasure, the observer might be the supervisor, the instructor conducting a scheduled check, or a third party trained as an observer.

For the most part, if motor skills are the focus of a learning event, it is because they are a regular part of the participant's job and therefore can be readily observed when the participant is engaged in the job. Observing motor skills involves fewer problems with sporadic use and less concern with confidentiality than observing intellectual skills.

An exception is the measure of safety or emergency skills that cannot be observed in use. Data are collected on such skills in two ways. One is to hold a drill specifically for the purpose of evaluation. The second is to bring participants to an assessment site periodically to evaluate their skills.

On-the-job Measures of Verbal Information

Verbal information is generally used to support intellectual skills and is tested at the end of the learning event to determine areas in which additional learning is needed for the participants to be able to perform the intellectual skills. If the intellectual skills are being used on the job, it can generally be assumed that the verbal information has been retained.

If it is necessary to determine if verbal information has been retained, it is possible to simply re-administer the instrument that was used during the learning event.

On-the-job Measures of Attitude

Attitudes can be measured by observing behaviors that could be expected to result if the participant holds that attitude or by asking the individual about the attitude directly. It is not useful to ask others about an individual's attitude because others can only be certain of behavior. The decision tree in Figure 8-3 is made up of ten questions. Each will be discussed in turn.

1. Does the attitude result in measurable behaviors? In many situations, the organization is interested in an individual's attitude because attitude impacts behavior. For example, managers who believe that participation is the best management strategy will frequently involve employees in the decision-making process; similarly, employees who believe that quality is important will devise or utilize systems to check their own quality. In such situations it is possible to measure the frequency of the behavior.

2. Do existing records reflect use of the behavior? Bypassing data collection by using existing records certainly is the most cost-effective approach. Observable actions—such as absenteeism, complaints, or suggestions—may be behaviors related to attitude. However, HRD professionals need to avoid the temptation to rely on existing data whether or not they fit the attitude. The first step is to consider what behaviors are representative of a given attitude and the second is to determine if existing records yield that data. Reversing the process—that is, identifying existing data and assigning it as a measure of an attitude—generally yields poor results.

3. Is the participant likely to record the behavior honestly? If participants are likely to record behaviors honestly, data collection can be assigned to them as part of the learning process. If participants are likely to falsify reports of their behavior, either inadvertently or deliberately, then others can be asked to report on the behavior.

4. Is frequency the important consideration (self-reporting)? In some situations, the number of times a behavior is performed is

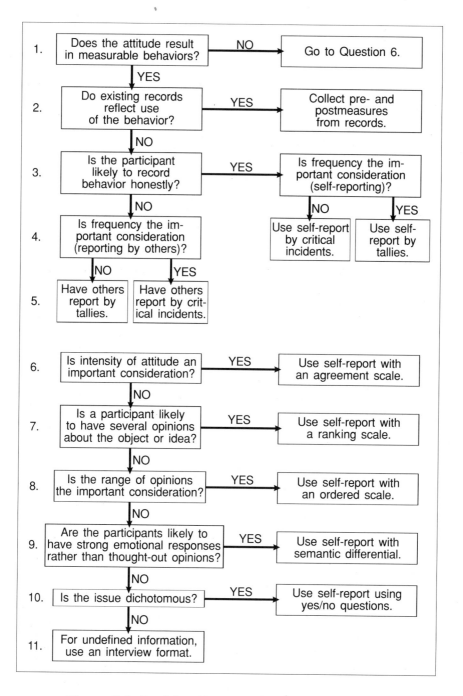

Figure 8-3. Decision Tree for Measures of Attitude

a measure of the attitude. For example, if keeping up with new technical information is the attitude, then the number of articles read or conferences attended might be an appropriate measure. In such cases, simple tallies are useful. In other situations, frequency is unimportant; it is more representative of the attitude that an individual responded appropriately when the occasion arose. For example, the behavior of taking customer needs into consideration might be measured by writing up one or more critical incidents that illustrate the attitude. Anecdotal reports are appropriate to measure behaviors for which frequency is not the major factor.

5. *Is frequency the important consideration (reporting by others)?* If others are asked to report on behavior, accounts can be obtained from peers, managers, and in some cases, subordinates. If frequency is a critical factor, then tallies are used; if not, anecdotal reports of critical incidents are used.

6. *Is intensity of attitude an important consideration?* When it is not possible to determine attitude from behavior, the only alternative is self-reporting by the individual. The disadvantages of using self-reporting include the following:

- The answer depends on the individual's self-awareness;
- Individuals are likely to answer the way they think others want them to answer;
- The provided responses may not represent the individual's attitude; and/or
- The individual may consider the responses too personal to reveal.

The promise of anonymity may alleviate only the second issue and thus does not eliminate the disadvantages. Nevertheless, if behavior cannot be measured, asking directly is the only recourse. Self-report measures of attitude have little meaning by themselves. They take on meaning only when they are used in a pre- and postlearning format or when they are compared to a norm.

A number of self-report techniques are possible; the choice depends on what the evaluator is trying to determine. The techniques include agreement scales, ordered scales, semantic differential scales, ranking scales, dichotomous scales, and interviews. If intensity of the attitude is an important consideration, agreement scales are appropriate. Agreement scales use the familiar format of strongly agree, agree, undecided, disagree, and strongly disagree.

7. Is a participant likely to have several opinions about the object or idea? When participants are likely to have several opinions, ranking can determine the relative weight of each viewpoint. Ranking scales list several statements, which participants order by rank. Reporting is usually done by number or by percentage of participants who ranked each item as first, second, or third.

8. Is the range of opinions the important consideration? If it is important to know how many participants support each different opinion, ordered scales are used. Each of the possible opinions is listed, and each participant marks the one that most closely represents his or her opinion. Percentages can be used to report the respondents who hold each opinion.

9. Are the participants likely to have strong emotional responses rather than thought-out opinions? If participants are likely to have strongly positive or negative feelings toward an object or idea, the semantic differential scale can be used. The semantic differential lists a series of adjectives and their opposites as poles of the scale.

10. Is the issue dichotomous? It is more common for factual issues to be dichotomous than it is for attitude issues; nevertheless, sometimes a simple yes-or-no response can be given. Reports then indicate the number or percentage responding to each of the two options. If the issues surrounding the attitude are too unclear to formulate questions, interviews can be used to gather data; these data can be used either to report findings or to formulate one of the tools discussed previously.

On-the-job Measures of Cognitive Strategies

Most learning events target specific knowledge, behaviors, or attitudes that the organization wants participants to use on the job to accomplish a specific organizational goal. Evaluation tools measure the extent to which that happened. Cognitive strategies, such as problem reframing, using analogies, and critical reflection, enhance participants' abilities to think and to solve problems across disciplines. The difficulty in measuring the on-the-job use of cognitive strategies is that the target cannot be specified. If participants learn to be better critical thinkers—that is, to reflect on the assumptions that guide their actions—the resulting behavior may be a creative new manufacturing process or a demand by supervisors that management address a reward system that thwarts cooperative action. Both would be evidence of the use of the skills, but the latter might be unanticipated or even unwelcome. As the preceding example illustrates, one measurement difficulty is in anticipating how such skills will be used. A possible technique is to ask participants, through individual or group interviews, to recall incidences of use. The results would not provide frequency information, but rather would provide data to indicate whether or not the skills were being put to use.

A second difficulty in evaluating the use of cognitive strategies on the job occurs because of the problem of measuring the quality of the thinking. For example, if an individual uses an analogy as a thinking tool, the analogy might range from worthless to extremely valuable; the same could be true with creative thinking and reframing problems. The worth of the product of the cognitive strategy is a matter of judgment, and often only the individual using the strategy has enough data to make that judgment. It is possible to ask participants if they have used such strategies, but less possible to determine if the strategies produced desired results.

When cognitive strategies are used to address a specific organizational problem, as might occur in quality circles or action learning sets (see Chapter 11), it is possible to measure the organizational gain from the activity. For example, Revans (1988) implemented action learning in ten London hospitals. Participants in the process learned to ask "fresh questions" about existing problems. One of several measurable results was a reduction in the length of patient stay.

PLANNING TO COLLECT USAGE DATA

The most critical factor in data collection is planning it well in advance of the learning event itself. In terms of the quality planning process (see Figure 8-4), the features to be measured are usage behaviors, not learning event measures. These features are established well in advance of the development of the product itself.

In a learning event, the progression of steps in collecting usage data is as follows:

1. Specify the on-the-job behaviors, knowledge, or attitudes that will solve the problem or meet the customer need.
2. Determine what data to collect on usage and from whom.
3. Establish criteria for quality requirements.
4. Determine the data collection process.
5. Develop data collection instruments or tools.
6. Field test instruments and processes.
7. Collect baseline data related to behaviors or attitudes.
8. Define course objectives related to those behaviors, knowledge, or attitudes.
9. Establish minimum criteria for performance.
10. Construct performance measures to determine whether participants can meet objectives.
11. Develop the content of the learning event to teach those objectives.
12. Deliver the learning event.
13. Administer the performance measures.

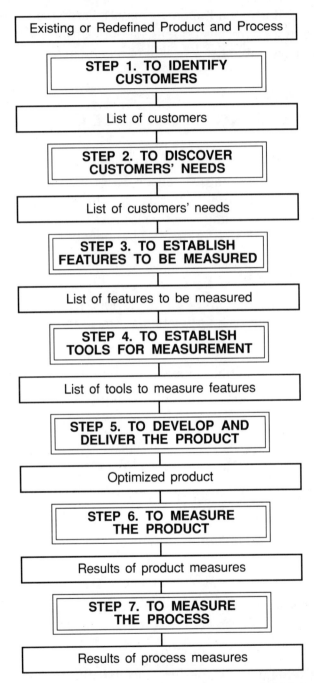

Figure 8-4. Steps in the HRD Quality-Planning Process

14. Remediate any participants who perform below minimum criteria.

15. Revise the learning event on the basis of the performance measures.

16. Repeat steps 12-15 until the learning event delivers satisfactory results.

17. Administer usage measures.

18. Analyze usage data.

19. Revise the learning event, remove contraints to usage, and improve coaching assistance.

20. Repeat Steps 12-19 until satisfactory results are obtained.

21. Construct reports of the usage data.

22. Determine whether the original problem has been solved or the original need met. If time and costs allow, it is helpful to collect more than one type of data on usage.

WHEN TO COLLECT USAGE DATA

A major concern with usage data is when to collect the information. In many cases it is necessary to collect data several times, particularly when the nature of the skill is such that it will increase or decrease with use. No set number of weeks or months can be established as ideal for the first data collection. One rule of thumb is to collect the data at the earliest interval after the learning event when (1) it could be expected that most participants would have had an opportunity to make use of skills that are employed only sporadically, and (2) the use has had time to impact others or to produce results. For example, if the content were presentation skills and participants averaged one presentation a week, three months might be an appropriate data-collection interval. It is not always necessary to collect all the data in one administration. For example, if the content were the repair of a specific piece of equipment for which the need might not arise for several months, it might be most appropriate to ask for individual data following each repair rather than waiting a year to contact everyone involved.

PROBLEMS

A number of problems that result from employing performance measures were discussed in Chapter 6. Problems also result from collecting usage data. As with the earlier set of problems, if these are anticipated, it is possible to eliminate them or at least lessen their impact. The four groups of stakeholders impacted by the usage data are the HRD managers, the instructors, the participants, and the line managers.

The HRD Managers

Concern About Negative Results. When usage data are collected, it is possible that the results will be negative, meaning that little on-the-job use is being made of the learning. The likelihood of negative results is greater if the HRD department does not have a history of identifying customer needs or one of establishing and measuring customer requirements. As in measuring performance, the problem for the HRD manager is that negative results might be interpreted by line management as an indication of ineffectiveness, which might lead to budget cuts before the data could be used to make improvements.

One place to start collecting usage data is by dealing with the results of one or more learning events that might transfer readily. Such a learning event would have the following characteristics:

- Intellectual skills are taught, as opposed to verbal information or attitudes;

- The skills are employed in a limited number of differing situations on the job;

- Participants are a select or hand-picked group, as opposed to open enrollment;

- The skills are clearly a part of the job tasks of the select group; and

- Performance standards have been established and measured during the learning event.

A second strategy is to concentrate resources in one area so that a relatively quick improvement could be accomplished. The usage data should indicate ways to improve the learning event, to remove the constraints to usage, and to establish coaching needs. Utilizing this data, the HRD department should be able to show increases in usage that would be seen by line management as continuous improvement in quality.

A third alternative is to delay the collection of usage data until HRD can go through the quality planning process so that the likelihood of results being positive are increased.

Costs. As with other measures at the end of the learning event, the largest percentage of cost for usage data is for the personnel to collect and analyze the data. Zemke and Kramlinger (1988), borrowing from marketing, have estimated the costs of personal interviews at $30 to $40 per interview, telephone interviews at $5 to $30 per interview, and surveys at approximately $10 per person. Other costs, such as those for compiling anecdotes, can be directly tied to the participant's or manager's salary. Costs can be lessened by a number of strategies already discussed:

- Using external observers whose cost is lower than instructors or participants for observation, interviews, and so on;

- Using existing data when possible (records or products);

- Using managers to collect data when it could be considered a normal part of their supervising responsibilities;

- Establishing collection procedures initially rather than retrofitting collection to existing learning events; and

- Using samples rather than total populations.

The decision trees for selecting data-collection techniques employ these factors as criteria.

Instructors

Need to Redesign Learning Events. Instructors are often surprised at how difficult it is to think through what on-the-job usage could be expected from a learning event. Many learning events have been designed from the point of view of "what they need to know" rather than "what they need to do." Instructors, if they are serving as experts on the subject matter, may be defensive about the way learning events have been constructed or at least dismayed at the amount of revision needed before usage measures can be put into effect.

Of the four stakeholder groups, instructors have the most difficulty accepting evaluation, because much of the obligation for instrument development, data collection, learning event revision, and so on, falls to them. Providing instructors with assistance in the form of evaluation expertise is helpful, but does little to lessen the burden.

Participants

Discomfort with Being Observed. An unexpected observer who shows up to watch an employee work can be disconcerting. Employees may be concerned about why they are being singled out, or how other employees will interpret the observation. A like situation can occur with interviews. Even surveys can be intimidating if they appear suddenly.

The most appropriate time to prepare participants for the collection of usage data is at the time of the learning event. In many cases it is possible to even distribute the data collection instruments for participants to view and to discuss.

Who Will Receive the Data. A second concern is who will receive the data and whether participants will be reported on individually or as a group. This is a concern whether the data refer to the participants themselves or whether the data are collected on subordinates, peers, or supervisors. The data-collection instrument itself needs to indicate how the data will be used. As a rule of thumb, data are reported back to those from whom they are collected. If managers find they are providing data but seldom hear results, they may tend to regard the data as unimportant.

Line Manager

Fear of Revealing Negative Management Practices. Managers are sometimes concerned that the data collection will reveal negative information about themselves. They may also be concerned about who will have access to the data. The most effective way to deal with line manager concerns is to get prior agreement about what is to be measured and how. If managers, as customers, have specified their needs and have helped to establish the requirements, they are more amenable to the measurement process.

Employee Time Away from Work. Managers express concern that the data collection procedures will take employees away from work to talk to interviewers, to fill out surveys, to write up anecdotes, and so on. In some cases it is possible to use a sample rather than the entire population to collect data. It is also unnecessary to collect data on usage each time the learning event is held. Once the HRD department answers its initial three questions (see page 89) and is on its way to increasing on-the-job usage of learning, periodic measures may be all that are needed for maintenance.

Evaluation for Retention[2]

Measures of retention, like measures of usage, are employed after the learning event. These measures determine the accuracy with which the skill is being performed. Many skills decrease in accuracy over time, particularly skills that are practiced infrequently or for which performance feedback is not available. The amount and type of initial practice has an effect on the length of retention of the skill. Thus, based on retention data, an HRD professional may choose to lengthen or shorten the learning event.

Retention is evaluated for the following two reasons: (1) to improve the learning event by adjusting the amount of practice and (2) to determine the point at which relearning should occur to maintain skill accuracy. As an example of the need for relearning, retention data may show that employees can perform CPR skills at an acceptable level for up to six months after their training, but then need a refresher course if the skills are to be maintained.

Four conditions affect the length of time skills are retained: task difficulty, task importance, task frequency, and feedback.

TASK DIFFICULTY

Rose (1985) classifies tasks as difficult, moderately difficult, and easy. A task is considered to be difficult if it has the following characteristics:

[2]The author gratefully acknowledges the assistance of Paul Nichol in the preparation of this chapter.

- A number of items or concepts that need to be considered at any one time;
- More than ten independent steps that need to be performed in order;
- Several decision points with numerous options;
- Close error tolerance requiring considerable hand-eye co-ordination; and/or
- No job aid.

A task is considered moderately difficult if it has these characteristics:

- Simple concepts following logical rules;
- More than ten steps that can be performed in any order;
- Several simple two-path decisions;
- Moderate error tolerance requiring some hand-eye coordination; and/or
- A job aid that acts as a memory jogger.

A task is considered easy if it has these characteristics:

- Less than ten steps;
- No branching; and/or
- An excellent job aid that contains all the information necessary to do the task correctly.

For example, a difficult task is maintaining a complicated piece of equipment that has a small error-tolerance and requires complicated trouble-shooting to determine the cause of the malfunction. A difficult task requires part-task buildup (separating the task into small, easy-to-learn portions and spreading the learning over time) to achieve the first correct performance of the task. Difficult tasks are subject to a high rate of skill decay; in very difficult tasks, decay can occur before the end of the initial training.

In contrast, a moderately difficult task does not require the careful buildup needed for a difficult task, but it does require practice to sustain required proficiency. An easy task, especially one that is performed often and has built-in or provided feedback, can be taught with a simple "explain-demonstrate-imitate" routine. Easy tasks, after initial correct performance, do not require much practice and the rate of skill decay is usually very low.

TASK IMPORTANCE

A task is considered to have high importance if, when not done or done improperly, it can result in death, serious injury, or substantial loss of revenue. A task is considered to have moderate importance if, when not done or done improperly, it can result in injury or impair successful job accomplishment. A task is considered of low importance if, when not done or done improperly, it can result in hardship, but will not significantly impair successful job performance or result in injury.

Task importance is measured by the consequence of inadequate or improper performance on the job. For a recruiter, the task of interviewing would be of moderate importance because poor skills would lead to hiring unqualified employees.

TASK FREQUENCY

A task is considered to have high frequency if it is performed on the job on the average of once every two weeks. A task is considered to have moderate frequency if it is performed on the job at least once every eight weeks. A task is considered to have low frequency if it is performed on the job less than once every eight weeks.

Low frequency of performance can result in skill decay. This is especially true for difficult tasks. On the other hand, high frequency of performance maintains skills and can even lead to skill enhancement. An exception is when the skill is performed incorrectly or poorly; under such circumstances, frequent execution can decay performance. For this reason feedback on performance is vital to sustaining proficiency regardless of how often the task is performed.

FEEDBACK

Feedback can come from the task itself or from others' reporting on the skill. The most effective and usually the most accurate feedback is from the task itself, such as when a machine begins to function again after being repaired. In many situations the task cannot provide feedback; for example, for writing skills, the employee must depend on feedback from others. In some situations the feedback arrives too late to be useful, such as when the skill is interviewing.

Figure 9-1 displays four configurations related to feedback. In each diagram, the horizontal line represents correct performance. The longest vertical line indicates the end of the learning event, and subsequent vertical lines indicate the passage of time.

Diagram A illustrates a situation in which a skill has been learned to the correct level of performance during a learning event. When the skill is not used again, decay occurs. Although delay is not a problem for easy tasks, it is a significant problem for difficult tasks that have substantially steeper decay curves. Such tasks are particularly prevalent in maintenance; personnel may be trained to repair a specific piece of equipment and then encounter a long delay before the equipment needs repair. Another example would be employees who have been trained for complex emergency or disaster procedures, but for obvious reasons have had no opportunity to use the skills.

In Diagram B the skill has also been learned to the correct level of performance by the end of the learning event. In this situation the skill is employed frequently but the performer receives little or no feedback on the success of the performance. The decay curve illustrates that the frequent use of the skill helps to sustain proficiency, but the lack of feedback causes the skill to decay gradually over time. This diagram represents what happens to managerial skills for which little feedback is provided. It also

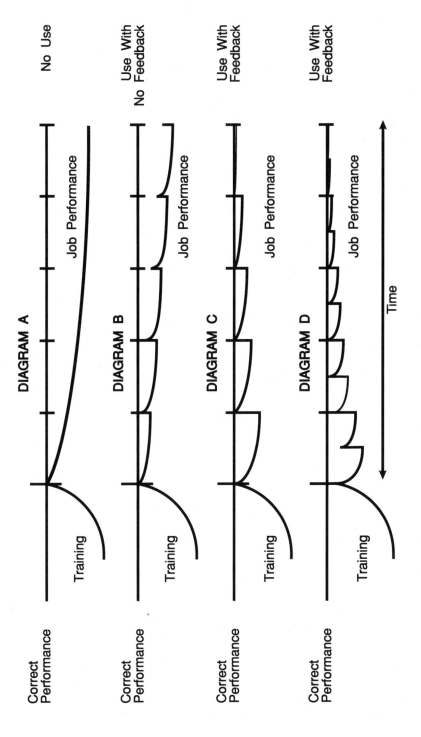

Figure 9-1. Task Training and Retention—Job Performance Factors

illustrates the situation of many assembly-line workers who find themselves doing the same task repeatedly, but who receive little feedback on their performance other than data on the speed at which they produce.

Diagram C represents the most favorable scenario: a skill that is used often on the job and on which the performer receives regular feedback on how well the skill was performed. Each use reinforces the skill and sustains proficiency. If the skill is employed frequently enough, at some point skill decay would virtually stop as the function became automatic.

Diagram D provides an example of an easy or moderately difficult task that is performed often on the job, but for which accurate initial performance is not critical. Because the skill is used frequently and provides feedback, and because the training need only familiarize the participant with the skill, greater speed and proficiency can be attained on the job. Word-processing skills, for example, would fall into this category. If the skill were to be used frequently and provided feedback, but also had to be performed proficiently the first time on the job, more training would be required in the initial learning event—a costly proposition.

Decisions about the amount of practice, spacing, and degree of proficiency needed to perform the skill are determined by a task analysis conducted before the learning event is planned. Retention data provide feedback that allows curriculum designers to revise and to fine tune the learning event based on the reality of on-the-job conditions. When a skill is overtrained the result is wasted time and money, as well as participant boredom. When a skill is undertrained, the skill may be unusable, discouraging, or in some cases, dangerous. Timing for the initial measure of retention takes into account frequency of use and the extent to which the skill was learned to proficiency during the learning event.

TRAINING STRATEGIES

Retention is affected by the training strategy used. Training strategies can be categorized as single session, double session, progressive, and comprehensive.

Single Session. A single training session with the task performed at least one time correctly. Job-quality proficiency is attained on the job.

Double Session. Two separate training sessions with correct performance achieved in each. Job-quality proficiency is attained on the job.

Progressive. A series of three training sessions with correct performance, including job-quality proficiency, by the last training session.

Comprehensive. A series of three to five training sessions with correct performance achieved in each training session and job-quality proficiency attained by the last session.

PREDICTED PROFICIENCY

The second reason for measuring retention is to determine the point at which relearning needs to occur. Tables have been computed for this purpose; however, they provide only general guidelines that need to be adjusted by actual measurement. Table 9-1 provides average decay rates for tasks classified as having high, medium, and low levels of difficulty. The table was constructed by Paul Nichol (1989), co-author of this chapter, using a task-retention model developed from a United States Army Research Institute study on training-task repetition and retention (Hagman, 1980). The first column, Training Session, lists four training strategies. The second column rates task difficulty using the AIR (Rose, 1985) categorization methodology, which is further described in Figure 9-2, pages 123 through 125.

As shown in Table 9-1, an individual prepared in a single session on a task with a high difficulty level can retain the skill for up to two weeks without performing it, and still be at 89-percent proficiency. Using a progressive technique, the same skill could be retained for four weeks at the 89-percent proficiency level. The

Table 9-1. Predicted Proficiency of Task Performance over Time

Training Strategy	Task Difficulty	Weeks Since Last Performance — Predicted Proficiency																									
		1	2	3	4	5	6	7	8	9	10	11	12	13	14	15	16	17	18	19	20	21	22	23	24	25	26
Single Session	High	94	89	84	79	75	71	67	63	60	56	53	50	47	45	42	40	38	36	34	32	30	28	27	25	24	22
	Medium	99	97	96	95	93	92	91	89	88	87	86	85	83	82	81	80	79	78	77	76	75	74	73	72	71	70
	Low	99	99	98	97	97	96	95	95	94	94	93	92	92	91	90	90	89	89	88	88	87	86	86	85	85	84
Double Session	High	96	93	89	86	83	79	76	74	71	68	66	63	61	58	56	54	52	50	48	46	45	43	41	40	38	37
	Medium	99	98	97	96	95	95	94	93	92	91	90	89	89	88	87	86	85	85	84	83	82	82	81	80	79	79
	Low	100	99	99	98	98	97	97	97	96	96	95	95	94	94	94	93	93	92	92	91	91	91	90	90	89	89
Progressive	High	97	94	92	89	87	84	82	79	77	75	73	71	69	67	65	63	61	60	58	56	55	53	52	50	49	47
	Medium	99	99	98	97	97	96	95	95	94	93	93	92	91	91	90	89	89	88	88	87	86	86	85	85	84	83
	Low	100	99	99	99	98	98	98	97	97	97	96	96	96	95	95	95	94	94	94	94	93	93	93	92	92	92
Comprehensive	High	98	95	93	91	89	87	85	83	81	79	77	75	73	72	70	68	67	65	63	62	60	59	58	56	55	54
	Medium	99	99	98	98	97	97	96	95	95	94	94	93	93	92	92	91	91	90	89	89	89	88	88	87	87	86
	Low	100	99	99	99	99	98	98	98	98	97	97	97	96	96	96	96	95	95	95	95	94	94	94	94	93	93

training proficiencies apply to first performance after the initial training. Once on-the-job performance has occurred, all prediction should be read from the comprehensive row.

The table can be used to estimate the timing for data collection to determine retraining needs. Because the measurement is of proficiency and not amount of usage, either observation or product evaluation are employed.

---

1. Are job or memory aids used when performing the task?

Answer	*Weighted Value*
- Yes	1
- No	0

2. How would you rate the quality of the job or memory aid?

Answer	*Weighted Value*
- Excellent. Using the aid the entire task can be accomplished with no additional information or help.	56
- Very Good. Using the aid, a performer would need only a little additional information to complete the task.	25
- Marginally Good. Even with the aid, important additional information would be needed to accomplish the task.	2
- Poor. Even with the aid, a great deal of additional information is needed to accomplish the task.	1

3. How many steps does it take to complete the task? (For the purpose of this rating, a step is a separate physical or mental activity within a task that has well-defined, observable beginning and ending points. It must be performed to complete the task correctly.)

Answer	*Weighted Value*
One step	25
- Two to five steps	14
- Six to ten steps	12
- More than ten steps	0

Figure 9-2. Ten Questions That Determine Task Difficulty

4. How many of the steps in the task are required to be performed in a definite sequence?

Answer	Weighted Value
- None	10
- All	5
- Some	0

5. Does the task provide built-in feedback so you can tell if you are doing each step correctly?

Answer	Weighted Value
- Has built-in feedback for all steps	22
- Has built-in feedback for most steps (half or more)	19
- Has built-in feedback for some steps (less than half)	11
- Has no built-in feedback	0

6. Does the task have a time limit for its completion?

Answer	Weighted Value
- No time limit	40
- Has a time limit, but it is easy to meet	35
- Has a time limit and it is difficult to meet (more often the reason for failure than improper performance)	0

7. How difficult are the mental processing requirements of the task?

Answer	Weighted Value
- Almost no mental requirements	37
- Simple mental processing requirements	28
- Complex mental processing requirements	3
- Very complex mental processing requirements	0

Figure 9-2 (continued). Ten Questions That Determine Task Difficulty

8. How many facts, terms, names, rules, or ideas must be memorized to do the task?

Answer	*Weighted Value*
- None (or a job aid provides all the necessary information)	20
- A few (one to three)	18
- Some (four to eight)	13
- Many (more than eight)	0

9. How hard to remember are these facts, terms, and so on?

Answer	*Weighted Value*
- Not applicable. There are none or they are all provided by a job aid.	34
- Not hard. The information is simple.	31
- Somewhat hard. Some of the information is complex.	12
- Very hard. The facts, terms, and so on, are technical or specific to the task and must be remembered in exact detail.	0

10. What are the motor control demands of the task?

Answer	*Weighted Value*
- None	2
- Small but noticeable degree of motor control	0
- Considerable degree of control	16
- Very large degree of motor control	3

The weighted values are added together to produce a total rating score:

99 and less	= Very Difficult
100 to 139	= Moderately Difficult
140 and above	= Not Difficult

Figure 9-2 (continued). Ten Questions That Determine Task Difficulty

Stopgap Measures of Usage

The techniques suggested in Chapter 8 to measure usage demand a great deal of preparation before the learning event occurs—or much backtracking to put the pieces into place. This chapter provides several stopgap techniques to measure usage. These techniques cannot substitute for the more carefully planned measures; they are far less effective for revising the learning event itself or for increasing on-the-job usage. They can, nevertheless, serve as a stopgap, if measures are needed while more systematic processes are being put into place.

NEEDS ASSESSMENT MODEL FOR CONDUCTING FOLLOW-UP STUDIES

The first stopgap method was developed by Borich (1980) for assessing preservice and inservice training for teachers. The method, based on discrepancy analysis, examines what the learning event intended to accomplish versus what participants perceive was actually achieved on the job. Borich's method has been somewhat modified here for use in organizational settings.

The first step in the process is to construct a list of the competencies that the learning event is intended to teach. If measurable objectives exist, they can be copied directly. However, they should be checked against the activities and materials to be sure the objectives represent the actual learning. If objectives do not exist they can be derived from the participant and instructor materials and from the activities of the learning event.

The competencies next are listed on a form like the one shown in Figure 10-1. Category titles can be altered depending upon the need; for example, alternative categories might be "knowledge of the principles" and "perceived relevance."

The instrument is administered to the total population or to a sample at a specified time after the learning event. Participants rate each of the competencies on a five-point scale. The difference between Column 2, "Perceived Importance," and each of the two columns that follow is calculated for each respondent as shown in Figure 10-2.

Competency	Perceived Importance to Job	Ability to Perform Competency	Ability to Produce Results Using Competency
1.	1 2 3 4 5	1 2 3 4 5	1 2 3 4 5
2.	1 2 3 4 5	1 2 3 4 5	1 2 3 4 5
3.	1 2 3 4 5	1 2 3 4 5	1 2 3 4 5
4.	1 2 3 4 5	1 2 3 4 5	1 2 3 4 5
5.	1 2 3 4 5	1 2 3 4 5	1 2 3 4 5
6.	1 2 3 4 5	1 2 3 4 5	1 2 3 4 5

Key: 1 = Low
2 = Moderately low
3 = Average
4 = Moderately high
5 = High

Figure 10-1. Form for Discrepancy Analysis of Usage Versus Intent

Column 1	Column 2	Column 3	Column 4
Competency	Perceived Importance to Job	Ability to Perform Competency	Ability to Produce Results Using Competency
1.	1 2 3 ④ 5	1 2 ③ 4 5 = 1	1 ② 3 4 5 = 2
2.	1 ② 3 4 5	1 ② 3 4 5 = 0	① 2 3 4 5 = 1
3.	1 2 3 4 ⑤	1 2 3 ④ 5 = 1	1 2 3 ④ 5 = 1
4.	1 ② 3 4 5	1 2 3 ④ 5 = -2	1 2 3 ④ 5 = -2
5.	1 2 ③ 4 5	1 2 3 ④ 5 = -1	① 2 3 4 5 = 2
6.	1 ② 3 4 5	1 2 3 ④ 5 = -2	1 2 3 ④ 5 = -2

Key: 1 = Low
2 = Moderately low
3 = Average
4 = Moderately high
5 = High

Figure 10-2. Scores of Participant A

Next, the average importance score across all respondents is calculated for each competency as in Figure 10-3. The results of these calculations are useful to understand the perceived importance of each competency and to weight the individual responses on each of the additional columns.

The averaged score for importance for each item (Column 2) is multiplied by each respondent's discrepancy score for the item to produce weighted totals. The results of this step for Participant A are shown as Figure 10-4.

The calculated scores for each competency are then totaled and averaged to produce a weighted score for each competency for

Participant	Perceived Importance of Competency 1 to Job
A	1 2 3 ④ 5
B	1 ② 3 4 5
C	① 2 3 4 5
D	1 2 3 ④ 5
E	1 2 ③ 4 5
F	① 2 3 4 5
G	1 2 ③ 4 5
H	1 ② 3 4 5

Average = 2.5

Figure 10-3. Participants' Responses to Competency One

Column 1	Column 2	Column 3	Column 4
Competency	**Perceived Importance to Job**	**Ability to Perform Competency**	**Ability to Produce Results Using Competency**
1.	Average = 2.5	1 x 2.5 = 2.5	2 x 2.5 = 5.0
2.	Average = 4.0	0 x 4.0 = 0.0	1 x 4.0 = 4.0
3.	Average = 3.0	1 x 3.0 = 3.0	1 x 3.0 = 3.0
4.	Average = 1.5	-2 x 1.5 = -3.0	-2 x 1.5 = -3.0
5.	Average = 2.0	-1 x 2.0 = -2.0	2 x 2.0 = 4.0
6.	Average = 3.5	-2 x 3.5 = -7.0	-2 x 3.5 = -7.0

Key: 1 = Low   4 = Moderately high
2 = Moderately low   5 = High
3 = Average

Figure 10-4. Scores of Participant A

Participants	Competency					
	1	2	3	4	5	6
A	2.5	0.0	3.0	-3.0	-2.0	-7.0
B	0.0	2.0	-1.0	3.0	4.0	3.0
C	2.0	3.0	1.0	5.0	3.0	3.0
D	1.0	3.5	0.0	4.0	5.0	2.0
E	3.0	1.0	1.5	5.0	3.0	4.0
F	2.0	2.0	-3.0	3.0	5.0	3.5
G	1.0	3.0	-7.0	2.0	4.0	2.0
H	3.0	4.5	0.0	5.0	4.0	4.5
Total	14.5	19.0	-5.5	24.0	26.0	15.0
Average	1.8	2.4	-0.7	3.0	3.3	1.9

Figure 10-5. Ability to Perform Competency

both "ability to perform" and "ability to produce results." Figure 10-5 shows the results of this calculation for "ability to perform." The highest positive scores are those which should receive priority for revision. On the basis of this analysis, competencies 4 and 5 need the greatest attention to help participants perform the competencies on the job.

Figure 10-6 (page 132) shows a sample final composite chart.

This method is superior to the more typical post-learning-event questionnaires in two ways. First, it does not employ simple averages, which tend to eliminate differences, resulting in totals

Competency	Perceived Importance to Job	Ability to Perform Competency	Ability to Produce Results Using Competency
1.	2.5	1.8	2.8
2.	3.0	2.4	3.4
3.	1.5	-0.7	-0.5
4.	4.0	3.0	1.0
5.	4.5	3.3	4.7
6.	2.0	1.9	3.9

Figure 10-6. Composite Chart

that are not very useful. Second, it asks participants to respond to actual competencies, rather than the more general question "Were you able to use what you learned?" Further, it asks for that response in terms of both use and results, so that the response is more helpful for revision.

The needs assessment model for follow-up studies provides data for improving the learning event and for coaching for increased usage. However, the model depends on the participants' self-assessments and is thus subject to many of the problems discussed in Chapter 3.

THE SUCCESS CASE

The second stopgap technique is the success case proposed by Brinkerhoff (1983). It consists of several in-depth case studies rather than a determination of how all participants have used the learning.

The technique involves selecting a small number of participants from the learning event. Those selected should be participants who have been implementing the learning successfully. The selection may be the result of telephone calls to a sample of participants or the hunches of the instructor based on the level of enthusiasm displayed during the learning event. Random selection is not the focus, because it is a "successful" population that is sought, not an average one.

Having identified possible cases, the evaluator collects in-depth data by interviewing the participant, by interviewing peers or others involved, and examining existing records. Brinkerhoff (1983) suggests the following five interview questions:

1. How have you used the training?

2. What benefits can be attributed to use of the training?

3. What problems did you encounter in using the training?

4. What were the negative consequences of the training and/or its use?

5. What criteria did you employ to decide if you were using the training correctly or incorrectly?

Conclusions drawn from the interview should be investigated and supported with evidence from other sources, records, corroborating interviews, and so on. The data are analyzed as in case studies. Therefore, the analysis process is reported along with the conclusions. Reports can take the form of individual case studies, themes that all cases have in common, or cost/benefit estimates.

Brinkerhoff suggests using this method for learning events with broad appeal but unclear outcomes; for new learning events that are experimental or are still being tested; or in situations in which there is not time for the use of more systematic measures. The major drawback of this approach is that it does not represent what the average participant may have gained from the program. Its major benefit is that it allows an in-depth look at on-the-job usage, providing much richer data than other forms of data collection would afford. In so doing, it yields data on how the learning event could be improved. When data are needed to demonstrate effectiveness to others, the success case method provides quick and nearly guaranteed results.

ACTION PLAN AND AUDIT

The third stopgap measure is use of action plans developed during the learning event and systematically audited at specified later dates. Evidence indicates that having participants set goals to be accomplished back on the job increases the use of skills from the learning event.

The process of participants' constructing action plans is familiar to most instructors. Typically, the last portion of the learning event is set aside for participants to think through the specific steps in an implementation plan. Frequently the plan is shared with other participants to get further input.

Although action planning itself is a fairly common instructional technique, auditing the plan is much less common. If the organization has a history of having participants complete action plans that are not audited, it may be difficult to convince participants to take the planning seriously.

Several modifications to action planning make it more useful for evaluation. A form, in triplicate, can be provided for the final draft of the plan. On completion of the learning event, the participant takes one copy, the participant's manager is sent the second copy, and the instructor retains the third copy. Figure 10-7 shows a typical form with these five columns:

1. The action that is to be taken;

2. The need or purpose for the action;

3. The date by which the action is to be completed or measured;

4. What will serve as evidence of the accomplishment; and

5. A numerical estimate of the accomplishment (savings, decrease in number of safety violations, increase in number of statements of positive reinforcement given to subordinates, and so on).

Participants are encouraged to think in terms of goals that can be accomplished within one to three months. If longer-term goals are selected, the plan can be broken down into smaller steps, some of which can be accomplished within a three-month time frame. The instructor or evaluator constructs a list of the completion dates on each of the participant's forms. Each participant is contacted in person or by telephone approximately two weeks after the specified date. Copies of the participant's original action-planning form are used to guide the discussion. The purpose of the call is to obtain answers to the following questions:

- Has the action step been completed? When?
- What was the evidence of the accomplishment?
- What is the numerical value associated with the accomplishment?
- What difficulties were encountered in accomplishing the goal?
- In what other ways have the skills, knowledge, and attitudes been used in the interval since the learning event?

The responses are noted on the form and a copy is forwarded to the participant's manager. When all participants have been audited the responses are compiled.

The major drawback to this technique is that it provides no data to indicate that the goals would have been accomplished without the learning event. In fact, participants tend to write goal statements about tasks they had already planned to accomplish. The major benefit is that it provides numerical data on an individual basis, rather than attempting to prove total organizational results, which may be considerably harder to establish.

Action Item	Purpose	Date	Evidence of Accomplishment	Numerical Value

Figure 10-7. Action Plan

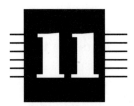

Evaluation and
Management Development

Management development broadly refers to the learning events directed at managers in an organization. However, in most organizations those learning events are extremely varied and involve many types of learning outcomes (see Chapter 5).

One type of outcome in management development is verbal information. Examples of learning-event topics for managers that have verbal information as an outcome include information on policies and procedures, information on how the organization is doing financially, and theories of motivation or leadership. Management development that is primarily verbal information is evaluated with objective measures.

A second type of outcome in management development is intellectual skills; examples include how to use a personal computer, how to conduct financial analysis, how to use a specific decision-making model, and how to carry out a new set of procedures for a performance review process. Management development that has intellectual skills as an outcome is evaluated through performance demonstrations.

A third type of outcome is attitude; examples include the value of participative practices, an appeal for leadership, and taking personal responsibility. This type of learning is often measured by attitude surveys and questionnaires.

The fourth type of outcome is development. Although not one of the outcomes referenced by Gagné and Briggs (1979), it can be differentiated from the other outcomes discussed in Chapter 3. Development refers to a change in self-knowledge and a concomitant change in how one perceives and acts on the world. It implies a change in a positive direction, toward growth or maturity. Examples of management courses that have development as an outcome are displaying sensitivity to others, giving negative feedback in a way that reduces defensiveness, making empathetic responses to others, handling conflict, coaching others, and dealing with ambiguity. Management development often implies a learning outcome of this nature. This type of learning has also been the bane of evaluators. Development has proven bewildering to evaluate; when evaluation *has* been accomplished, the results have been generally discouraging.

RESULTS OF EVALUATION OF
MANAGEMENT DEVELOPMENT

Campbell, Dunnette, Lawler, and Weick (1970) conducted the major review of the literature on management development. After examining eighty-four studies published over the last two decades, they found no evidence that participating in training and development was related to success as a manager. In most cases this finding resulted from the fact that job performance was not measured. For example, thirty-five of the studies were attempts to produce an employee-centered attitude change in managers. Surveys administered to subordinates showed attitude changes in 80 percent of the cases, but the studies did not examine whether the attitude change influenced job performance.

Another group of five studies conducted with T-groups produced significant changes in about 20 to 25 percent of the participants in such areas as increased openness, receptivity and tolerance of differences, and increased skill in interpersonal relationships. The primary tools for determining change were open-ended questions asked of subordinates or associates a year after the laboratory experience. However, eight similar studies, which used measures of change administered to the participants themselves, showed no significant difference over control groups. With one exception, the T-group studies did not attempt to evaluate influence on job performance.

A third group of seven studies, which were concerned with problem solving and decision making, produced largely negative results in terms of improved job performance.

Looking more broadly at training and development, Campbell (1971) summarizes personal beliefs of what is known about management development:

> What do we know? We know that management development can change managers toward more employee-centered attitudes. We know that laboratory education probably can change behavior in the workrole, but the nature and implications of these changes are unclear.... We know almost nothing about what makes orientation, sales, or team training effective.... We know that technical training, as well as remedial training in basic skills, does produce significant increments in knowledge. (p. 593)

Goldstein (1980) reviewed the literature for the same publication nine years later. Although Goldstein found increased interest in evaluation, the results of the studies were generally the same. Other reviews of management development (Clement, 1981; Miles & Biggs, 1979) reached similar conclusions about the limited effectiveness of management development on performance.

An in-house study by Martelli (1987) examined the performance-appraisal ratings of twenty-three first-line supervisors in light of the amount of management training they had either during the previous twelve months or over their careers. This study's conclusion was that supervisory training did not have a significant influence on performance as judged by performance-appraisal ratings.

Two studies provide some explanation for why management development seems to have little proven effect on performance. The first, conducted at Honeywell (Zemke, 1985), concluded that 50 percent of what a manager needs to learn was gained from job experiences and assignments; 30 percent was learned from relationships with supervisors, peers, consultants, and upper-level managers; and 20 percent resulted from training.

In a second and more extensive study of executive development in six corporations, Lindsey, Homes, and McCall (1987) tied specific learnings to a range of developmental events. The thirty-four leadership qualities they identified as typical topics of development (for example, dealing with conflict, comfort with ambiguity, stress, uncertainty, using-not-abusing power) were not learned from courses but from such on-the-job experiences as assignments, projects, and personal failures. Course work was a factor in learning only the following five leadership qualities:

1. Specific technical knowledge;

2. Problem solving and problem framing;

3. Management models and theories;

4. Self-confidence in skills and abilities (a result of being selected for prestigious programs); and

5. Perspective on life and work (gained from hearing other participants' points of view).

After three decades of studies on management development, a discouraging but realistic picture is emerging. The difficulty of proving the effectiveness of development courses may not lie in ineffective measurement techniques; it may be that development courses simply produce so little change in performance that no appreciable difference results. It may be time for HRD professionals to consider the fact that they can effectively teach managers verbal information, intellectual skills, motor skills, and even attitudes, but that development is not learned in a typical course or workshop.

Brush and Licata (1983) reviewed the literature on the effectiveness of managerial training to examine the "learnability" of managerial skills. They conclude that:

Most managerial skills are comprised of knowledge and behavioral components which interact with noncognitive variables. To the extent that noncognitive and social-interactive factors play a large and critical role in the skill, there is less probability that an individual weak in this particular skill will become competent through training. (p. 36)

Several management theorists (Argyris, Putnam, & Smith, 1985; Revans, 1980; Schon, 1987; Weick, 1983) would support that position. Vaill (1989) builds a strong case against considering managerial competencies as techniques to be taught, holding that all competencies are interwoven with the here-and-now perceptions of the manager, which are deeply rooted in character and personality. Vaill asks, "What bet are we making when we teach competencies without dealing with this deeper phenomenon?" (p. 38).

Yet this separation of action and self is what occurs in most management development courses. A three- or five-day course with twenty-five managers provides neither the time nor a suitable environment in which to delve into the personal values and beliefs of the managers. Rather, the courses are designed to teach managers competencies or skills that are viewed as being separate from the individual's belief system. The difficulty that arises when such actions are stated as competencies is they become intellectual skills that are rule directed, rather than responses to interactions. For example, two typical competencies follow:

- "The listener will be able to reflect back to the speaker the underlying feelings expressed in the speaker's statement."

- "The manager will be able to establish trusting, dependable relationships with subordinates."

Most employees have interacted with managers who attempt to implement rule-directed responses learned in a training course. Typically, they recite stock phrases, such as "What I hear you saying is…." Or they implement standard processes, such as first give praise, then give corrective feedback, and then end with praise. The employee's response to such rule-governed interaction is to feel manipulated. The recipient of the phrases or processes often notices an incongruity between what is said and what the receiver intuitively feels is believed by the manager. Interpersonal interactions reflect who the individual is; to separate the two leads to phony interactions.

Without a corresponding belief system to guide the interaction, managers have only standard phrases or processes in their repertoires. They have trouble inventing new responses for unfamiliar situations. A typical sequence is for the manager to try the skills for a few days and then revert to former, more comfortable, responses.

Thus, although development skills can be described in measurable statements and although they can be taught and even measured at the end of a learning event, they do not constitute development. Nor do they appear to have a lasting effect.

PROCESSES THAT LEAD TO DEVELOPMENT

Development results from on-the-job experiences as illustrated in the Lindsey et al. (1987) and Zemke (1985) studies. Development can also result from purposeful learning experiences, but only if learning and work are integrated. Development does not occur in isolation from real life. McCall et al. (1988) make the following point:

> An individual can demonstrate an ability only when the job demands it. The ability to come up with a workable and strategic agenda is only tested when a manager has sufficient scope of responsibility and the latitude to establish a direction. One's values aren't demonstrated until one faces a dilemma that forces action either consistent or inconsistent with a value. The ability to cope with ambiguity is difficult to assess in an unambiguous job; how one will handle a mistake is hard to know until a mistake is made. (p. 166)

The conditions for management development in the work environment appear to be as follows:

- The manager is engaged in a real work problem that is personally meaningful;

- Someone (peer or facilitator) or something (feedback from the results) challenges the way the manager is thinking about the problem; and

- The experience occurs over time so opportunity is available for both action and reflection.

The challenge to HRD professionals is to create new ways to help managers develop—ways that bring learning and work closer together, rather than treating learning as a separate event. An obvious way to begin is to make better use of job assignments and on-the-job experience. McCall et al. (1988) provide suggestions aimed at executive development, but many of the processes are equally appropriate for the development of all managers.

Several development processes that blend work and learning have gained acceptance in the last few years. Often, however, these initiatives have come from line management, not HRD. Examples are action learning (Revans, 1980), action science groups (Argyris et al., 1985), and participative action research (Whyte, 1989). Each of these processes is briefly described here, not as answers, but as illustrations of formats that merge work and learning.

Action Learning

Action learning, as pioneered by Revans (1980), is a management development process that has been implemented widely in Europe. Managers take on problems that provide them with challenges. In some situations the challenge is to work on an unfamiliar problem; for example, a production manager may try to solve a problem in human resource development. In other situations the problem is familiar but the organization is unfamiliar, such as when a marketing manager for a chemical company examines a marketing problem in a bank. As they work on the problems over a period of several months, the managers meet weekly in small groups (usually four to six members) to discuss the problems they are trying to resolve. Revans refers to the members as "comrades in adversity." Groups are often made up of individuals from differing departments or organizations to add new perspectives through which the members can hear and challenge one another's assumptions.

Development occurs as managers learn more about themselves through the results of their own actions and the challenges of their comrades. The payoff to the organization is creative solutions to difficult problems that have resulted from applying a fresh perspective.

Action Science

Action science, as developed by Argyris (1985), involves managers' meeting with a facilitator trained in "Model II" skills, for two purposes: (1) to resolve a difficult business problem on which the group or individual feels stuck, and (2) to try to understand what "defensive routines" exist in the group or organization that prevent the resolution of such problems. This second understanding Argyris calls "double-loop" learning. For an in-depth look at the problems, group members construct mini-cases that describe their attempts to resolve the problems. A specific set of strategies—Model II—is modeled by the facilitator and practiced in the group to help members examine the cases and uncover the group's defensive routines. Again the payoff is twofold: managers learn about themselves and the unproductive ways they may be interacting, and the organization gets a thorny problem unblocked.

Participative Action Research

Participative action research is based on the work of Lewin and influenced by sociotechnical analysis and work-place democracy. Selected members of an organization, representing various functions, meet together over a period of months to diagnose a significant organizational problem, to collect data, and to implement a solution. The process is guided by a researcher skilled in action research processes. The results are threefold: development of the individuals involved, a solution to an organizational problem, and research data that adds to the literature on how organizations function. In reporting on the individual development that resulted from a participative action research project at Mondragon in Spain, Santos (1989, p. 578) notes "the development of a more open mindset, the explicit awareness of diversity in the system, the will to arrive at the root of problems, the enhanced capacity to listen and get beyond the obvious, [and] the development of a greater capacity for analysis and reflection."

EVALUATION OF DEVELOPMENT

In each of the preceding examples, three results can be measured: the effectiveness of the process, the development of the individual manager, and the organizational results.

The self-knowledge that is learned in development is unique to each individual. That uniqueness makes the outcome of development unpredictable and the use of predesigned questionnaires or checklists unpractical. The learning can however be described by the individual in case studies, logs, critical incidents, interviews, and so on. The data then can be analyzed through qualitative evaluation approaches to determine the overall effectiveness of the specific development approach.

The manager of the individual involved in the development process has the responsibility for determining if that individual has become a more effective manager as a result of the development process. As Jaques (1989) notes:

> Personal effectiveness appraisal is one of the prime acts of a manager.... [It] is the manager's judgment of how well a subordinate did in achieving a given output, with the shifts and changes that were imposed and with all the other unexpected and unplanned-for circumstances that inevitably arise in the course of working. How well (or how badly) a subordinate has done is a matter of pure judgment—and always will be a matter of judgment—and should be accepted as such. (p. 103)

Yet, it is possible for managers to make such judgments both for purposes of evaluating the learning process and evaluating the individual.

Finally, when learning and work are integrated, as they are in the three methodologies discussed previously, there is a direct organizational benefit. For example, an action learning project involving ten London hospital resulted in a quicker recovery rate for patients (Revans, 1980). A participative action research project implemented at Xerox resulted in a cost savings of 3.2 million dollars in their wire-harness department (Whyte, 1989). The third evaluation for each of these integrated processes is the return on investment in terms of problems solved.

SUMMARY

The following conclusions can be drawn about evaluating management development:

- Human resource development professionals have been successful in producing results and in measuring those results when the learning outcomes of management development are verbal information, intellectual skills, or attitudes.

- Human resource development professionals have been less successful at both producing and measuring results when the learning outcome is development.

- Evidence indicates that development occurs when managers take action in real work situations and their thinking is challenged by the results of their actions or by their peers.

- Human resource development professionals need to create new formats for development that integrate learning and work.

- Development is evaluated through the qualitative analysis of descriptive reports from managers themselves, performance appraisal from the manager's supervisor, and organizational outcomes.

Making Decisions About Learning in the Organization

Making decisions about how much and what kind of learning will go on within the organization requires answers for the following three questions:

1. Are the skills, knowledge, and attitudes employees gained useful to them on the job?
2. What skills, knowledge, and attitudes currently reside in the organization?
3. What is the relationship between the cost of employees' learning the skills, knowledge, and attitudes and the benefits the organization receives from that learning?

The first question was dealt with at length in Chapter 8. Chapter 12 addresses the second question and Chapter 13 addresses the third.

RECORDING SKILLS, KNOWLEDGE, AND ATTITUDES

If the end product of human resource development is defined as a skilled and knowledgeable work force, then HRD professionals need ways to measure accumulated skills, knowledge, and attitudes within the organization. Most HRD departments keep records of which employees attend each learning event and transfer that information to personnel records. Typically, if employees attend learning events, their records are updated automatically regardless of whether or not they learned the competencies established. Because such records reflect attendance and not learning, they are of little use to management as a source of information about the skills, knowledge, and attitudes (SKA) that currently exist in the organization.

Performance measures implemented in learning events, as outlined in Chapter 5, make it possible to determine and to record accurately participants' gains in skills, knowledge, and attitudes. Beyond the use of such measures as an indication of HRD's effectiveness, such a database has the potential to provide the organization with information needed for manpower planning, assessment of learning needs, and the identification of candidates for jobs that require specific skill sets. As pay-for-skill is increasingly applied in organizations, this database becomes a repository for records and the measurement tools become means of verifying skills.

Two methods are suggested to record that a participant has successfully met the established performance criteria. The simplest method is to use the existing system, but to record attendance only if the participant has met the criteria established. If participants do not achieve competence, their attendance simply is unrecorded.

The second method is to create a new database using one indicator for having attended a course and a different indicator for having met competence. This method allows HRD to compile a record of attendance for courses not related to the job, as well as to compile records of skills, knowledge, and attitudes.

If such a database were developed, participants' managers would be able to review the records. Some HRD professionals are concerned that managers might use the information to make salary or promotion decisions. As disquieting as this idea is initially, in reality management sends an employee to a learning event to gain certain skills, knowledge, and attitudes. If the employee fails to meet the minimum criteria agreed on by management and HRD, then management has a right to know. Otherwise a manager may wrongly assume that the employee has obtained the sought-after SKA and plan accordingly. The basis on which a manager would choose to reward or promote the employee is a managerial decision. If the manager has created a pay-for-skill compensation system, it may very well be appropriate to reward those employees with newly acquired skills. However, such a system would be unfair to participants and their managers, and of little use to the organization, unless the six conditions set out in Figure 12-1 were met. Each of those conditions will now be examined in turn.

1. Measurement tools have been validated.
2. Management has specified minimum competence.
3. Participants have been informed that competence will be measured.
4. Alternative ways to meet minimum competency have been established.
5. Prerequisites are enforced.
6. Record specifies that participants have met or have not met competence, not their relative scores.

Figure 12-1. Conditions for Reporting Participant Learning

1. Measurement tools have been validated. This first condition is the most important. It would be unfair to report a participant's SKA if the measurement tools were not valid and reliable. Whether the tool is an objective test, performance measure, project, checklist, rating scale, product scale, or some other tool, HRD professionals must be able to show that the tool is valid (that it measures what it purports to measure) and that it is reliable (that it is consistent). If tools have not been subject to rigorous validation procedures, their results should not be reported.

2. Management has specified minimum competence. The level of competence needed for a particular SKA is established through discussions with management. If this dialog has not taken place then HRD has no basis on which to determine minimum criteria.

3. Participants have been informed that competence will be measured. When comprehensive evaluation is first introduced in an organization, participants may not anticipate that they will be measured, much less that the results will be available to management. For this reason, participants should be informed of the measures in advance through course descriptions and enrollment procedures. The advance information allows participants enrolled in an event as a break from the workday routine to change their minds. Certainly at the start of any learning event, the instructor should inform participants (1) how they will be measured, (2) the minimum criteria for competence, and (3) who will receive the results.

4. Alternative ways to meet minimum competency have been established. The intent of measuring competence is not to sort employees into groups as "competent" and "incompetent," but to guarantee a product. Therefore participants need feedback about their performances and opportunities to relearn and try again to meet competence without penalty. In some cases, this process may occur within the learning event itself; in other cases it may occur after the learning event.

5. Prerequisites are enforced. If participants and instructors are to be held accountable for learning the skills, knowledge, and attitudes presented at the learning event, then entering participants must have the prerequisites that will make success possible.

6. Record specifies competence, not relative scores. Any record should indicate only that the participant has or has not met competence rather than specific scores on the performance measure.

ADDITIONAL CONSIDERATIONS

HRD is not the only place for employees to gain skills, knowledge, and attitudes. Employees also may attend universities, external workshops, or conferences, or they may read on their own. If the database is to accurately reflect the SKA in the organization, employees need ways to demonstrate what they have learned. This can be accommodated by placing performance measures, which have been developed for learning events, in a central location. The location may be an actual site or a holding bank from which materials are distributed. Such a location can also serve to administer premeasures that allow potential participants to avoid sitting through a learning event whose content they have already mastered.

If a participant is unable to meet the minimum criteria established for competence, then he or she should have the opportunity to try again to demonstrate performance at a future date and to have the competence recorded. How the relearning occurs depends on the situation. If the participant has met virtually none of the criteria for SKA, attending the learning event a second time might be a viable option. However, if the participant is close to meeting criteria, other options might be more cost effective. A few possibilities are suggested in the following list:

- Partnering participants who need help with other participants who are particularly knowledgeable about the content;

- Holding follow-up sessions with the instructor for those who need further help;

- Providing self-paced packages that can be sent to the participant or that are housed in a learning center;

- Tutoring of individual participants at their work sites by the instructor;

- Learning from employees at the work sites who have already developed the SKA; and

- Coaching by the participant's manager.

Once the SKA have been obtained, participants need the opportunity to demonstrate performance. Here again the possibilities vary from situation to situation. Suggested methods are as follows:

- Provide the participant's manager with the performance measure for administration;
- Create a central location with tools on file to which employees can go to demonstrate SKA; and/or
- Have instructors visit each site on a regular schedule both to tutor employees and to administer performance measures.

Costs/Benefit Analysis

What is the relationship between the cost of employees' learning and the benefits the organization receives from that learning? The following three models are useful in examining this question further: (1) cost comparison; (2) causal model; and (3) return on investment. Although the models differ considerably, the first step in each is to determine the cost of the learning event.

DETERMINING COSTS OF LEARNING

The term *learning event* includes courses, but also encompasses less traditional forms of learning. The cost of a learning event is computed by simply adding all its associated costs. Ways to categorize costs have been suggested by a number of authors. Kearsley (1986) suggests using the categories of personnel, equipment, facilities, and materials. Head and Buchanan (1981) propose five categories: student costs, instructional costs, facilities costs, administrative costs, and instructional development costs. Swanson and Gradous (1988) also suggest five categories: analysis, design, development, implementation, and evaluation.

The particular categorization chosen is probably less critical than the thoroughness with which the detail in each category is included. The two variables discussed here are each-time costs and one-time costs. *Each-time costs* are usually associated with the learning event itself, and the costs are incurred each time the learning event is given. *One-time costs* are associated with the design, development, and revision of the learning event. Each-time costs include the following:

- Participant salaries;
- Participant travel;
- Participant lost-opportunity costs;
- Instructor salary;
- Instructor travel;
- Facilities (classrooms, learning center);
- Materials (participant materials, instruments);
- Equipment (video, overheads, computers); and
- Registration and record-keeping costs.

One-time costs include the following:

- Needs analysis;
- Subject matter expertise;
- Development of materials;
- Development of evaluation tools;
- Pilot and revision costs;
- Administrative costs;
- Graphic artist's time; and
- Clerical time.

Some of these costs will be defined in the following paragraphs.

Participant salary is calculated on a per-day basis, averaged for the level of employee attending the learning event. Fringe benefits generally add 35 percent to an employee's salary, and overhead costs are estimated at 125 percent of salary plus benefits. In most organizations employees work 230 days in a year.

Assuming an average salary of $40,000 for the participants, the cost per participant-day would be calculated as follows:

Salary	$40,000
Benefits (@ 35% of salary)	+14,000
Subtotal	$54,000
Overhead (@ 125% of subtotal)	+67,500
Total	$121,500
Divided by number of days	÷ 230
Per-day costs per participant	$528

Cost per participant-day = $528 x Number of participants

Participant travel includes travel, lodging, per diem, and so on.

Participant lost-opportunity costs represents what the participant would be expected to contribute to the organization if he or she were not involved in the learning event at that time. This amount is calculated when learning events are held as separate from work. Increasingly, however, learning and work are integrated; for example, an internal organizational development consultant will help a group work more effectively together while they are engaged in a real task. When work and learning are integrated there is no need to calculate lost opportunity costs nor the participant salary costs discussed previously.

Instructor salary and *instructor travel* are calculated in the same way that participant salary and travel are calculated.

Facilities represents the cost of the location of the learning event, usually estimated in cost per square foot of floor space, again divided on a per-diem basis. Often this information can be obtained from the accounting or facilities department.

Materials refers to consumables, those materials that will be used up each time the learning event is given, such as participant manuals, performance measures that are completed, and computer time.

Equipment used for instructional purposes such as overheads, video equipment, and flip charts are estimated on a per-diem basis over the life of the equipment. The life of most equipment is not more than five years. A 10-percent maintenance figure should be added to the calculations for equipment.

Registration and record-keeping costs for a particular event include clerical help to send out notices, distribute participant materials, prepare rosters, duplicate materials, and so on.

The one-time costs listed above are generally development costs associated with the initial preparation and revision of the learning event. The total is divided by the estimated number of times the learning event will occur. That figure is added to the total of the each-time costs calculated above.

The *needs analysis costs* should include the salary of the instructional designer conducting the needs analysis as well as the cost of employees who are interviewed, who complete forms, and so on. Evaluation costs are calculated in the same way. The exception is when the data collection process does not interfere with the ongoing work of the employee (such as observation) or when the evaluation utilizes processes that add value to the task (such as process-control charts). Under such circumstances additional employee costs need not be included.

THREE COST MODELS

Cost Comparison

The first model is *cost comparison*. Here the cost of one approach is compared with the cost of the second approach, such as in the following examples:

- The cost of an on-site learning event as compared to satellite delivery;

- The cost of a learning event held this year as compared to the cost of the same event last year;
- The cost of developing a learning event in-house as compared to the cost of purchasing it from a vendor; or
- The cost of providing a learning event as compared to the cost of doing nothing.

Cost comparison is computed by using two columns to add the figures and then comparing the totals. The last item on the list, the cost of providing a learning event compared to the cost of doing nothing, is an important comparison to make. As paradoxical as it seems, in some situations the cost of the learning event is greater than the savings or profit to be derived from the learning. In other situations, calculating the cost of doing nothing provides compelling evidence that ignoring the problem would be extremely costly to the organization. Swanson and Gradous (1988) provide a useful model for forecasting cost.

Causal Model

Some behaviors that participants learn in a learning event and subsequently use on the job have an impact on certain business indicators. However, the behaviors do not bear a one-to-one relationship to that business indicator. Because many other factors impact the same indicator, it is unclear whether an improvement in the business indicator can be attributed to the use of the new behaviors. In the same way, if no improvement in the indicator occurs after a learning event, it is unclear whether the learning event had any impact at all.

Sales training is an example of such a behavior. Many factors influence increased sales, including competitors' price changes, anticipation of new products, service records, and the sales techniques of the organization's sales representatives. If sales representatives receive training in new techniques and sales subsequently improve, it is open to question whether the training increased the sales or whether the increase resulted from some other factor.

It is, however, possible to build a chain of logic that increases the likelihood of determining if the increase can be attributed to the change in behavior. The logic chain involves the following ten steps:

1. Determine what behaviors differentiate successful performers from unsuccessful performers. This step is accomplished by identifying individuals representing both ends of the spectrum and then analyzing their behaviors (Castle, 1989; Spencer, 1983).

2. Select a group of participants to be trained in those behaviors which have been determined to differentiate the two groups.

3. Identify a like group of individuals who will not be trained or who will be trained at a later date (control group).

4. Collect baseline data on the rate of current use of those behaviors in both groups.

5. Note baseline data on the business indicator associated with the behavior for each individual or for the two groups.

6. Conduct the learning event to teach the differentiating behaviors to the participant group.

7. Measure performance at the end of the learning event to determine if participants can demonstrate the behaviors.

8. Collect usage data on the job to determine the rate of use of the differentiating behaviors in both groups.

9. Note any change in the business indicator for each individual or both groups.

10. Draw a conclusion about the relationship of training to the business indicator. Depending on the results, a number of conclusions could be drawn, some of which are listed in Figure 13-1. The most positive conclusion is the first one; such evidence would be compelling that the behavior impacted the results.

Example 1

	Behavior	Business Indicator
Participant group	Increases	Improvement
Control group	No increase	No improvement

Conclusion: The use of the new behaviors impacted the indicator.

Example 2

	Behavior	Business Indicator
Participant group	Increases	Improvement
Control group	No increase	Improvement

Conclusion: Either the use of the behaviors does not impact the business indicator or some other factor impacts it strongly enough to wash out the effects.

Example 3

	Behavior	Business Indicator
Participant group	Increases	No improvement
Control group	No increase	No improvement

Conclusion: Either the use of the behaviors does not impact the business indicator or some other factor impacts it strongly enough to wash out the effects.

Figure 13-1. Effects of Participant Behavior on Business Indicators

If any step of the logic chain is not developed, the argument loses its strength. For example, without evidence that the participants are using the differentiating behaviors more after the training than before, there is no way to tie the training to the increase.

Kearsley (1986) assigns percentages to steps in a causal model to arrive at a dollar figure. For example, assume the annual sales volume for a company is $200,000. The sales manager estimates that 50 percent ($100,000) of sales performance can be attributed to sales skills. If the training program produces a 50-percent increase in the use of differentiating sales skills, then a 25-percent (.50 x .50) increase ($50,000) might be anticipated in sales. If the cost of the training is $10,000, then an anticipated benefit of $40,000 can be assigned to the training. Clearly, the accuracy of the amounts assigned to the causal percentages impact the accuracy of the prediction.

The causal model is useful for a wide variety of business indicators that are difficult to tie to dollar amounts, such as absenteeism, number of grievances, performance ratings, and morale. However, for the causal model to be useful, it is necessary to show that the behavior being taught is used more by successful performers than by unsuccessful performers as measured by a particular business indicator. Unfortunately, much of the content of learning events is untested in this regard. Instructors will teach a theory that makes intuitive sense, but there is often little evidence that the theory works.

Return on Investment

The third model is *return on investment*. Using the term *return on investment* in HRD is controversial, because it has a specialized meaning in accounting. However, it has gained general acceptance in HRD; it will be used here to mean the ratio of the cost of the learning event to the dollar benefits.

The return of investment model is employed when the behaviors involved in the learning event bear a one-to-one relationship to the business indicator, so that the cost and return can be expressed in the same units, namely dollars. Human resource development can impact dollar amounts in two ways: increasing volume or decreasing expenses (Spencer, 1983). Increasing volume means teaching skills that increase the number of units produced. However, most of the benefits from HRD come from decreasing expenses. Spencer classifies decreasing expenses into five categories: time, materials, equipment down-time, retention/turnover costs, and people/problem events. Return on investment is calculated as follows:

$$\text{ROI} = \frac{\text{dollar amount from increasing units or decreasing expenses}}{\text{cost of the learning event}}$$

A ratio greater than one is positive.

In each of the three models, assumptions and estimates are necessary, because accurate data are unavailable or are too costly to obtain. For example, determining the exact salary of each participant in the learning event (rather than using an estimate of the average salary of employees at that level) may do little to increase the accuracy of the input data. Estimates and assumptions are legitimate as long as the basis for them is specified and they are spelled out in the report.

Profile of Characteristics of Learners

Several of the preceding chapters have dealt with the tools used to determine the extent to which participants gained skills, knowledge, and attitudes (SKA) from the learning event and the extent to which those SKA are used on the job. This chapter looks at the same issues from the perspective of "Who has learned how much from the learning event and who has put it to use in what ways?" Profiling learners is a way to understand the customer better by finding out information such as the following:

- What categories of customers are missing from learning events? What departments, ages, levels of employees?

- What categories of customers benefit most and least from the learning event?

- In what ways do different categories of customers use the learning on the job?

- What categories of customers make the most and least use of SKA on the job?

The graphs and correlations that result from these data can be used for the following purposes:

- To improve the learning event;

- To improve the selection process;

- To determine what follow-up is needed;

- To determine what new SKA are needed; and

- To determine what new methods for learning in the organization are needed.

A number of illustrations of what such data might reveal are provided in the following list:

1. As a result of a workshop on presentation skills, managers are able to apply 90 percent of the skills they have learned, but technical personnel can apply only about 40 percent of the skills. How can the learning event or the selection process be improved?

2. Data indicate that less than 10 percent of technical employees who have been in positions more than five years attend learning events provided by HRD. It is important to try to understand that missing customer. How are these populations staying current in their fields? Through conferences? Technical journals? What does HRD need to do to facilitate their learning?

3. Usage data for a learning event on time management indicate that if the new information is not implemented within the first two weeks following the learning event, it will not be implemented at all. What kind of follow-up can be used to encourage use within that time frame?

4. Data show that first-time managers implement a greater percentage of the skills they gain in a course for new managers if the learning event occurs between the third and sixth month that they are in their new job.

5. The dropout rate on a satellite-delivered program that has eight parts is lessened by 50 percent if the participants meet initially with a facilitator to discuss the program and exchange names and phone numbers.

6. Teamwork skills that are taught to intact work groups result in a significant difference in (1) members' willingness to share leadership of the group, (2) the level of decisions made, and (3) the length of meeting time. No significant

difference can be found for groups in which only one or two members of the group attend similar learning events.

7. Performance measures from a learning event indicate no difference between participants who attend voluntarily and those who have been "sent" by their managers. However, usage data show a significant difference in the extent to which the skills are used on the job.

8. Usage data for a learning event related to process control charts indicate that providing participants with calculators that they can keep increases the number of flow charts produced by the participants when they return to work by 25 percent over participants who are not allowed to keep the calculators.

These descriptions of possible results of profiling participants illustrate that there is not a generic list of categories for collecting profile data. The data that need to be collected are unique to each situation. Nevertheless, the major consideration in the analysis of participant profiles is the choice of characteristics to profile. Perhaps the most useful categories are based on the hunches of HRD professionals about the learning. For example, an instructor might notice that females rarely attend the learning event on leadership and decide to collect data to determine if the hunch is accurate. Profiling characteristics is a kind of detective work. The evaluator can search for meaningful data randomly, but the search is more fruitful if it is based on a good hypothesis.

Not all data for the participant profile need come from the same source. Some information can be asked in questionnaires administered well in advance of the learning event. Questions can be asked on the enrollment form, as a part of the premeasure, as a part of the performance measure, obtained when collecting usage data, or obtained from personnel records. It is, however, critical that all the information on an individual participant be coded in the same way in a database—for example, by employee number or social security number—so that data from varying sources can be related.

Data available from personnel records might include the following:

- Department;
- Level in the organization (job title);
- Length of service in the organization;
- Length of service in position;
- Shift; and
- Level of education.

In some organizations it may also be possible to obtain pre-employment scores for tests of reading level or English language skills. In many cases it is necessary to ask questions of the participants directly, such as who instigated their participation or whether they completed the pre-work.

Profiling participants is a part of the process of continuous improvement for HRD. Typically HRD professionals have not collected sophisticated data to improve service to the organization. Instead, they have relied on simplistic measures such as participant response forms or gross measures such as cost per student-day. One lesson HRD can learn from manufacturing is that unless the measurement tools are sophisticated enough to detect the error, the error will not be corrected. Using profile data to make comparisons about learning and usage lends increased sophistication to the measurement of HRD error and thus allows for much greater improvement in service.

Performance Demonstrations

Performance demonstrations are used as performance measures for both intellectual and motor skills. They are employed at the end of a learning event to determine whether or not the skills have been learned. They also serve as measures of on-the-job usage. Evaluating a performance demonstration focuses on procedure, product, or some combination of the two.

For some performance demonstrations the skill can be judged by the product; the procedures that the participant uses to create the product are much less important. For example, an instructor can judge how well participants produce mailing labels by asking them to produce a sheet of mailing labels as a final product; there is little need to observe the participants in the act of preparing the labels.

A product can also serve as the evaluation of the skill when a single correct answer results from the performance. Computing the rate of discount would be an example, as would accurately reading the settings from a micrometer.

However, for some performance demonstrations no product exists, such as in making presentations or responding to customer complaints. Here the skill is in the procedure rather than in the product, and it must be observed to be evaluated.

Finally, there are performance measures in which both the procedure and the product are important in judging the performance demonstration—such as landing an aircraft, for example.

It is generally less costly to judge a product than to observe performance because of the time involvement. Figure 15-1 lists several types of aids that can assist the evaluator in observing performance or evaluating the product.

Procedures

    Checklists
    Rating scales
    Performance samples
    Expert judgment

Products

    Right answer
    Rating scales
    Checklists
    Product samples

Figure 15-1. Measures for Performance Demonstrations

PRODUCT EVALUATIONS

Checklists

Checklists are dichotomous in nature, requiring a yes-or-no answer or indicating the presence or absence of a specific action or quality. A checklist could be used to indicate whether or not the participant put on safety goggles or typed a letter with a one-inch top margin. A column labeled "No opportunity to observe" is useful for observations; otherwise the absence of a check mark may wrongly indicate failed performance on an item that was simply not observed. Such a column is particularly helpful when an instructor is observing several participants at one time, or judging performance on the job where distractions may occur.

Because a checklist is dichotomous, it requires little judgment and therefore training is usually not needed. If a peer is to be asked to judge another's performance during a learning event, checklists are more appropriate than rating scales that require making judgments.

One special type of checklist, called the *Guttman Scale*, arranges items in a hierarchy so that each action depends on correct performance of the action listed before it. A single check mark would then indicate all the actions that had been taken to that point. For example, if the skill is to print a word-processing file, the steps might include the following:

1. Turns on computer;

2. Turns on printer;

3. Boots word-processing program;

4. Calls up file;

5. Gives print command; and

6. Prints file.

This type of checklist has an advantage over non-hierarchical checklists in that the evaluator can determine what has been accomplished by where the participant is in the process. In less hierarchical situations it would be unclear whether each of the steps had been performed. For example, a nurse could take the patient's temperature whether or not the thermometer had been cleaned first. Taking the temperature is not dependent on cleaning the thermometer—even though the steps should be accomplished in sequence. Not all checklists, however, lend themselves to the Guttman Scale.

In a learning environment it is important to do more than measure performance; it is also important to provide the participants with feedback for their continued learning. Checklists are particularly useful for feedback purposes. Yelon and Berge (1987) describe "fancy checklists" that are helpful to participants. *Fancy checklists* provide visual representations of the items on the list. Two illustrations (Figures 15-2 and 15-3) from Yelon and Berge's article illustrate this principle.

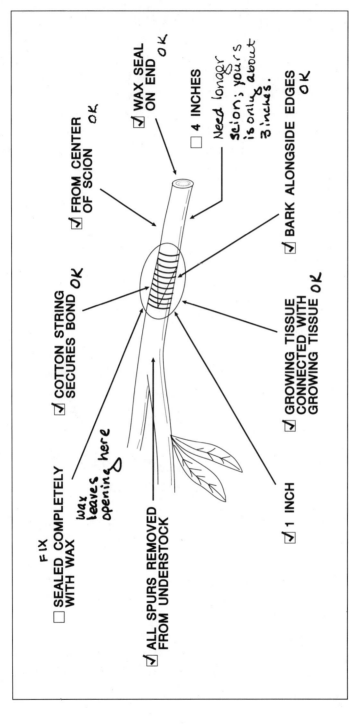

Figure 15-2. A Visual Checklist for a Product: A Good Graft[3]

Based on Crockett, J.W. (1977). *Crockett's Victory Garden*, Little Brown & Company, Boston, MA.

[3]From "Using Fancy Checklists for Efficient Feedback" by S. L. Yelon and Z. L. Berge, 1987, *Performance and Instruction, 26* (4), pp. 14-20. Copyright 1987 by National Society for Performance. Used by permission.

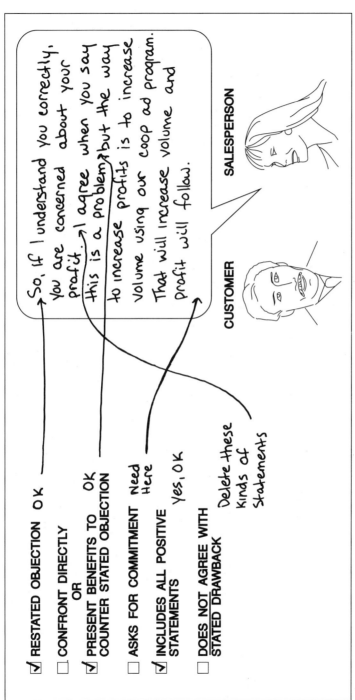

Figure 15-3. Excerpt from a Visual Interpersonal Skill with Highly Variable Responses[4]

[4]From "Using Fancy Checklists for Efficient Feedback" by S. L. Yelon and Z. L. Berge, 1987, *Performance and Instruction, 26* (4), pp. 14-20. Copyright 1987 by National Society for Performance. Used by permission.

A second technique that is helpful for providing participant feedback is to videotape the performance demonstration. With this technique it is helpful for the instructor to review the videotape with the participant some time after the course has ended or to make the tape available to the participant with the completed checklist.

Rating Scales

Rating scales consist of a graduated series of points of compliance rather than a simple yes-or-no response. Rating scales are appropriate if there is a degree of judgment in the performance, such as when one of the items is "arranges work space neatly." The quality of neatness is difficult to rate with a yes-or-no answer. Ratings are also needed when a series of observations is being summarized as opposed to a single incident; for example, in an interview a judgment as to whether the participant "made appropriate eye contact" would be summarized over the length of the interview.

There is some disagreement among evaluators as to whether an odd or even number of points on a rating scale is preferable. Those who prefer an even number of points on a rating scale hold that the absence of a neutral midpoint forces the observer to commit to a decision in one direction or another. Evaluators favoring an odd number of points on a rating scale hold that some respondents honestly do not have a preference on a given issue. If, under these circumstances, the evaluator forces the respondent to favor one side over the other, the resulting data will be less accurate.

The specific number of points used depends on the degree to which distinctions can be made between the points of the scale. If the distinctions are gross (such as poor, average, and good), then three points are adequate. If greater discriminations can be made with accuracy, then six or seven points can be used. Numbers larger than seven are generally not used because of the difficulty the observer has in holding more than seven distinct levels in mind at one time.

Although difficult to construct, scales with a descriptor at each point of the scale are more accurate than those with labels only at the poles. For example, if the product is a business letter, judgments may need to be made about its organization or style. In the following example, the skill being rated deals with writing paragraphs:

1	2	3
Lacks paragraphing and transitions	Some ideas are not adequately separated from others	Paragraphing acceptable, transitions clear

Another helpful addition to the rating scale is a blank space for comments by the observer. Even when the scaling points are well labeled, if judgment is involved, then the observer's comments can provide helpful feedback to the participant.

Two disadvantages of rating scales are that they are more subject to rater bias than checklists, and there is a tendency to rate all individuals at approximately the same position on the scale. For these reasons observer training is often required, making rating scales less useful for peer observation. Because the judgment made on rating scales is relative and not absolute, there is a need to establish criteria for competence, for example, at least four on the five-point scale.

Product/Performance Samples

Some products and performances are so complex that even checklists and rating scales are not adequate for evaluation. For example, handwriting exhibits this level of complexity. *Product/performance samples* allow a comparison of the product against carefully graded examples of varying quality and allow evaluators to deal with a high level of complexity. Three to five categories are constructed and given numerical values. Sample products/performances are identified for each category. The product/performance is compared to each sample and a judgment made as to which it resembles most closely. Sample products/performances may be produced specifically for evaluation purposes or have been saved from past learning events; the examples may be on videotape or exist in concrete form.

Expert Judgment

When a performance demonstration takes on a level of complexity beyond that which can be judged by product/performance samples—for example, an Olympic ice skating performance—a different strategy is required. In *expert judgment,* a panel of experts combines ratings. Even with the use of expert judgment, it is helpful to have rating scales to assist in the evaluation. Skills with this level of complexity in organizations might include counseling skills, elegance in design, and perhaps the charisma of leadership.

STEPS IN CONSTRUCTING THE PERFORMANCE DEMONSTRATION

Ten steps are recommended when constructing the performance demonstration. These steps are summarized in Figure 15-4 and are more fully discussed in the paragraphs that follow.

1. Identify the elements of the performance to be measured. Many performance demonstrations have so many elements that it is difficult to observe or measure all of them. An important first task is to use the Pareto principle to identify the vital few elements that make a critical difference in the performance.

2. Determine the level of reality that the performance demonstration can simulate. The goal is for the performance demonstration to model, as closely as possible, the situation in which the participant will actually perform the skill on the job. However, a number of considerations have to be taken into account in that decision: cost, availability of equipment, safety, and confidentiality. For example, in one organization, training was provided for a new system-wide software program for materials handling. The performance demonstration would have been most effective if partici-

1. Identify the elements of the performance to be measured.
2. Determine the level of reality that the performance demonstration can simulate.
3. Prepare the instructions for participants.
4. Determine how the performance demonstration will be evaluated.
5. Design the appropriate tools.
6. Review the form with experts in the subject matter.
7. Review the form with the customer.
8. Field test the form.
9. Identify the observers or experts.
10. Design the training for the observers.

Figure 15-4. Steps in Constructing the Performance Demonstration

pants could have actually signed on to the software program to demonstrate their skills. Unfortunately the design of this software was such that any data entered remained in the system for a period of seven months. Because it was unacceptable to have that much hypothetical data in the system for seven months, performance testing on-line was out of the question. Performance had to be demonstrated in a simulation of the real program that added considerable cost and lowered realism.

3. Prepare the instructions for participants. Constructing the instructions to the participants is a critical step in the process of designing the performance demonstration. The instructions need to state the conditions under which participants are to demonstrate their performance, including both constraints and assistance. For example, are there time limits? Can manuals be used for reference? Can help be sought from peers? What level of competence is required?

If on-the-job usage will be measured by performance demonstrations, it is important to inform the participants of this during the learning event. And, as discussed in Chapter 6, participants need to know who will have access to the results, both from the learning event and from data collected on the job.

4. *Determine how the performance demonstration will be evaluated.* Choose the measurement tool most appropriate for the evaluation. The tools include checklists, rating scales, product/performance samples, and expert judgment.

5. *Design the appropriate tools.* It is easy to underestimate the amount of time needed to create checklists, rating scales, and product samples. Not only is it an extremely time-consuming task, but the designer of the materials must have considerable knowledge of the subject matter to create the initial form.

6. *Review the form with experts in the subject matter.* Even if the form has been designed by experts, it is necessary to have other experts review the form for validation. The review entails consideration of the choice of items, their wording, their weighting, and the participant instructions.

7. *Review the form with the customer.* Customers also need to review the form because it will constitute the measure by which HRD's product is to be judged. The purpose of the customer review is to gain agreement on (1) the appropriateness of the vital few elements being measured and (2) the criteria established for competence. The criteria may simply be performing 100 percent of the steps or obtaining a minimum rating of 4.5 on the rating scale. However, in many cases more specific criteria need to be established. Gronlund (1988) provides a list of common standards for judging performance (see Figure 15-5).

8. *Field test the form.* The field test provides feedback on the instructions to the participant, the elements being measured, and the criteria. The checklist should be field tested with several individuals before being administered in a course for the first time. Even then the first few course administrations should be considered pilot runs from which revisions continue to be made. Not until

the form completes final revisions should the results be reported to anyone other than the participants, and they too should be informed of the stage of development of the form.

TYPE	EXAMPLES
Rate	Solve ten addition problems in two minutes. Type 40 words per minute.
Error	No more than two errors per typed page. Count to twenty in Spanish without error.
Time	Set up laboratory equipment in five minutes. Locate an equipment malfunction in three minutes.
Precision	Measure a line within one-eighth of an inch. Read a thermometer within two-tenths of a degree.
Quantity	Complete twenty laboratory experiments. Locate fifteen relevant references.
Quality	Write a neat, well-spaced business letter. Demonstrate correct form in diving.
Percentage Correct	Solve 85 percent of the math problems. Spell correctly 90 percent of the words in the word list.
Steps Required	Diagnose a motor malfunction in five steps. Locate a computer error using proper sequence of steps.
Use of Material	Build a bookcase with less than 10-percent waste. Cut out a dress pattern with less than 10-percent waste.
Safety	Check all safety guards before operating machine. Drive automobile without breaking any safety rules.

Figure 15-5. Some Common Standards for Judging Performance[5]

---

[5]From Norman E. Gronlund, HOW TO CONSTRUCT ACHIEVEMENT TESTS, 4e, © 1988, p. 92. Reprinted by permission of Prentice Hall, Inc., Englewood Cliffs, New Jersey.

9. Identify the observers or experts. Performance demonstrations can take considerable time during a learning event, particularly if the instructor must evaluate each participant personally. The time dilemma can be alleviated by using others to do the observation. This tactic has the added benefit of taking the instructor out of the role of judge and into the role of assisting the participants to prepare for the upcoming performance demonstration. Using the participants' supervisors as observers works to the HRD professional's advantage by involving supervisors in the learning process and preparing them for assisting with collecting usage data. Peers in the class can sometimes serve in the observer role, but only if the tools are checklists, and even then peers should not be the only observers. Other instructors, former participants, and contract employees can also serve as observers. The selection of observers depends on the level of expertise needed, the location, and the amount of training needed to prepare observers for their roles.

10. Design the training for the observers. No matter how well the checklists, rating scales, or product scales are designed, in the end they rely on the judgment of human beings, which is remarkably unreliable. The basis for poor reliability is the many types of errors humans can make, including the following:

- Misinterpretation: Words in the statement have different meanings to different observers.

- Inadvertent errors: Scores are added incorrectly or the observer's attention wavers.

- Lack of technique: Observers are unfamiliar with the form, or do not employ a systematic approach to observation.

- Conscious errors: The supervisor doing the rating does not want to make his or her employee look bad, or the instructor does not want to spend additional time reteaching a concept.

- Halo effect: There can be a tendency to think of particular participants as good at anything they do.

- Prejudice: Some observers tend to think certain classifications of participants will not perform well. For example, a rater might believe "ex-military supervisors just can't seem to feel comfortable with a participative style" and therefore rate such supervisors lower.

- Futility: Some people may believe that it does not matter how the forms are marked because the new skills will not make any difference.

The intent of observer training is to obtain individual accuracy and to achieve consistency across observer responses. Accuracy is improved with practice and with awareness of the types of errors observers may make. An effective technique to obtain consistency across observer responses is to have each observer complete the checklist for a product or procedure and then compare his or her results with those of others. If the data are to be useful for management's decision making, it is important not only that the observers be consistent within that particular group, but that they also be consistent with the way previous groups were rated.

MEASURING VERBAL INFORMATION THAT SUPPORTS PERFORMANCE

When the participant's performance demonstration does not meet the established criteria, the problem may lie in lack of skills or in lack of knowledge to support the skills. In some situations it is possible to determine from the performance demonstration which is lacking. However, in other situations, the determination is less clear. Under the latter circumstance, it is necessary to measure verbal information in addition to the performance. For example, if the participant is unable to troubleshoot an automobile engine within a given time limit, the evaluator must determine whether the difficulty lies in the specific procedure the participant is trying to follow or in lack of understanding of how combustion engines function.

A second consideration in determining whether both verbal information and performance should be measured is whether the skills being taught involve far or near transfer (see Chapter 8). When the competency involves far transfer, it is important to measure the participant's understanding of the principles that support the skill, even when the skill has been accurately demonstrated during the learning event. The measure of principles is necessary when far transfer is involved because it is not possible to ask participants to demonstrate all of the possible situations or conditions under which the skills will be employed on the job. Thus it may be that the participant performs the skill accurately in the situation that is constructed for the classroom demonstration, but is unable to apply the principles well enough to use them in situations on the job. For example, learning events that are designed to teach participants how to deal with customers more effectively often provide a series of steps or key actions to take. It is possible for a participant to accomplish all of the key actions in the proper sequence without understanding the basic principles. On the job, each customer and each situation is unique, necessitating that the participant invent new responses rather than recalling those that have already been learned. To invent a new response requires that the participant understand the principles that guide the selection of body language, timing, and/or choice of words.

By way of summary, Figure 15-6 provides a decision tree to help the HRD professional choose the most appropriate performance demonstration for the situation at hand.

This chapter has discussed the traditional tools for measuring the performance of intellectual and motor skills. As HRD professionals redefine their customers and reinvent their products, new tools of measurement also will need to be developed. Computer technology undoubtedly will play a large role in this future measurement. It is already possible for a computer to give immediate feedback on performance in many situations, such as the effectiveness of a design or the accuracy of an anticipated process. The future of performance measurement may lie in equipment that teaches at the same time it helps the learner to perform the task (Puterbaugh, Rosenberg, & Sofman, 1989).

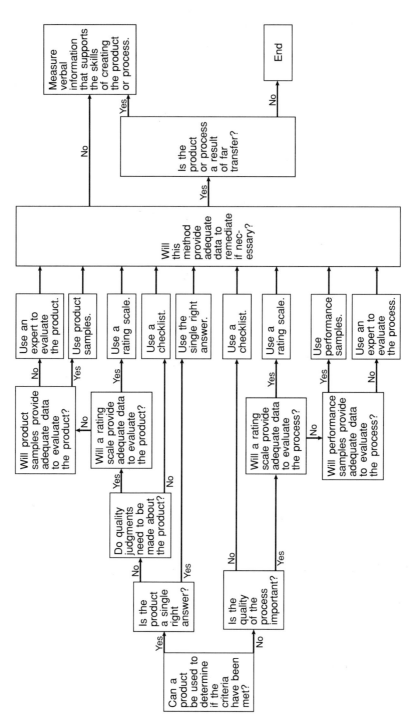

Figure 15-6. Decision Tree for Selecting Performance Measures

Constructing Objective Measures

Objective tests are primarily used to measure verbal information. They can also be used to measure certain kinds of intellectual skills (for example, mathematical calculations) or to measure other skills, such as when the participant executes the skill and then marks the appropriate response (for example, locating an error on a diagram). However, many intellectual skills cannot be measured by objective items, particularly those in which the performance must be observed, or the product must be rated.

Four kinds of items (individual questions with appropriate responses) are employed in objective measures: multiple-choice, true/false, matching, and completion items. Guidelines for constructing each type of item are listed below, along with the advantages and disadvantages of each.

GENERAL GUIDELINES FOR CONSTRUCTING OBJECTIVE MEASURES

Several guidelines for constructing objective measures are useful regardless of the type of item:

1. Arrange the items in order of difficulty; placing easier items first avoids discouraging participants unnecessarily.

2. Construct each item so that it is independent of all other items. A series of items in which the correct answer to the

first becomes the condition for answering the next item can prevent the measure from providing an accurate picture of the participant's knowledge or skills.

3. Avoid constructing items by taking quotes directly from a handout, overhead transparency, or book. Direct quotes tend to encourage memorization rather than understanding, and quotations taken out of context tend to be ambiguous.

4. Avoid trick questions. The intent of a performance measure is to determine the skills, knowledge, and attitudes of the participants, not to cause them to mark an item incorrectly.

5. As much as possible avoid negatives, especially double negatives. Such items take considerably longer to read and are often misinterpreted. If negative words must be used, underline or italicize the word or phrase to call attention to it.

6. Avoid providing clues to items in previous or subsequent items.

7. Use a variety of types of items in the performance measure rather than limiting the items to only one type. If the measure is lengthy, variety can add interest. When a variety of types of items are employed, group the items by type so participants do not have to constantly shift response patterns or reread instructions.

Multiple-Choice Items

Guidelines for constructing multiple-choice items are as follows:

1. The stem (the part that precedes the responses) should clearly state the premise; the response options should be kept as short as possible. For example, the following is considered a faulty item:

An income statement

a. reflects the firm's financial position.

b. is more important than the firm's balance sheet.

c. is a key financial statement.

d. is always performed on a cash basis.

The stem, "An income statement," fails to state the basis on which the response should be chosen.

2. The response options should contain only one defensible answer. If more than one item is correct, the effect of guessing is increased.

3. Distracters (incorrect responses) should be plausible; use common mistakes and misconceptions to create distracters. For example, the following is a faulty item:

Which element has been most influential in recent textile development?

a. Scientific research.

b. Psychological change.

c. Convention.

d. Advertising promotion.

Common sense would indicate that responses "b" and "c" are unlikely choices.

4. All response options should be grammatically and logically consistent with the stem; for instance, watch the uses of "an" and "the."

5. The length of correct responses should be approximately the same as the incorrect responses; there is a tendency to make the correct answer longer. For example, the following is a faulty item:

Plate current

a. never increases.

b. gradually increases.

c. increases to a point when the filament voltage is raised, provided the plate voltage is held constant.

d. is a measure of plate resistance.

6. It is more appropriate to ask what an item is rather than what it is not; knowing what is incorrect does not indicate

whether the participant knows what is correct. For example, the following is a faulty item:

The hurdle rate is not affected by

a. inflation.

b. interest rates.

c. cost of capital.

d. discount rate.

7. Include from three to five response options for each item. All items do not have to provide exactly the same number of response options.

8. "All of the above" is usually the correct answer and therefore makes the item too easy. The participant can guess "all of the above" is correct if two of the other options appear to be correct. For example, the following is a faulty item:

Which of the following factors are involved in achieving a defect-free product?

a. Quality.

b. Maintenance.

c. Personnel.

d. Supplier.

e. All of the above.

9. Rotate the position of the correct response from item to item. Instructors have a tendency to use "b" as the correct response more often than other response options.

10. Place any words that the response options have in common in the stem. For example, the following is a faulty item:

Interest rates are an important factor to consider in business cases because

a. interest costs are not deductible from income.

b. interest costs are not marginal costs.

c. interest costs are a component of the hurdle rate.

d. interest costs are a component of the discount rate.

The phrase "interest costs are" should be placed in the stem.

11. All options should be homogeneous in content. For example, the following is a faulty item:

The misery index

a. should be calculated for each project under consideration.

b. is calculated quarterly by the Chamber of Commerce.

c. looks at our balance of trade position.

d. may affect project viability in an indirect manner.

The first two responses refer to time, the third appears to be a definition, and the last refers to a consequence.

12. It is acceptable to use either a direct question or an incomplete statement as the stem. The preceding item used an incomplete statement. The following item uses a direct question:

Which type of data is used to express the number of defects found in a product at final test audit?

a. Categorical.

b. Numerical—discrete.

c. Numerical—continuous.

13. Use "none of the above" sparingly. It tends to test only the participant's ability to identify incorrect answers. Recognizing that items are wrong does not mean that the participant knows the correct answers.

Advantages of multiple-choice items include the following:

- Scoring is easy either by hand or machine.
- Unlike true/false or matching, multiple-choice items can measure varying degrees of correctness.
- Employing three to five response options reduces the effects of guessing which can be a problem with true/false items.
- Item analysis can be used to analyze and improve the items.
- Incorrectly marked response options are helpful to the instructor in diagnosing what misconceptions partici-

pants have; they provide a good basis for posttest discussion.

- They are considered by measurement specialists as the most versatile type of objective item.

Disadvantages of multiple-choice items include the following:

- They are one of the more time-consuming types of items to write; finding plausible distracters is particularly difficult.

- If poorly written, items can have more than one defensible answer.

- They are open to misinterpretation if participants read more into the item than is there; very knowledgeable participants may tend to overinterpret items.

True/False Items

Guidelines for constructing true/false items are as follows:

1. Have participants circle the correct answer rather than write in T or F. Poor or careless writing can make the letters "T" or "F" or even the words "true" or "false" very difficult to read.

2. Avoid the use of "always," "all," "never," "only," and "none"; these words alert the participant to mark the item false. For example, the following is a faulty item:

   T F   Effective managers always delegate.

3. Avoid the words "sometimes," "usually," "maybe," "often," and "may"; these words alert the participant to mark the item true. For example, the following is a faulty item:

   T F   The outflow section of the model is sometimes affected by the inflation rate.

4. If the statement is controversial, cite the authority whose judgment is referenced. For example, the following is a faulty item:

   T F The organization has a responsibility to provide assistance to employees who have drug problems.

   This statement as it is written appears to measure attitude rather than knowledge. To make it into a knowledge statement, it could be preceded by "The Federal Government has determined that..." or "The CEO has stated that...."

5. Do not include two concepts in one item. For example, the following is a faulty item:

   T F The trend toward quality circles began in the early 1980s and represents a big step forward in improving quality in the United States.

   Either of the two concepts, (1) began in the early 1980s or (2) represents a step in improving quality in the United States, could be false.

6. Each statement should be entirely true or entirely false without additional qualifiers such as "large," "regularly," "sometimes," and "may." For example, the following is a faulty item:

   T F No picture and no sound in a television set may indicate a bad 5U4G tube.

7. Keep true and false statements approximately the same length.

8. Have approximately the same number of true and false items. True statements are easier to write so there is a tendency to include more true than false statements.

9. Avoid making false statements by simply adding "not" to true statements. For example, the following is a faulty item:

   T F The binary number system is not a modernized version of the Arabic number system.

10. Avoid using trivial details to make a statement false.

11. Avoid a pattern of answers such as TTFFTTFF.

12. Place the central point of each statement in a prominent position or highlight it in some manner.

13. Avoid long and complicated statements that may test reading ability rather than the content. For example, the following is a faulty item:

T   F   If data are recorded to the nearest .001 inch (for example), then the class width should be an integer multiple of .001 inch so that each interval will contain the same number of possible data values.

14. Avoid negative statements and eliminate double negatives. For example, the following is a faulty item:

T   F   If a person has not had access to a patent, he or she cannot infringe the patent.

Advantages of true/false items include the following:

- The items can cover more material because they tend to be short.

- They take less time to construct than multiple-choice questions.

- Scoring is easier than with completion questions.

Disadvantages of true/false items include the following:

- They tend to emphasize rote memorization.

- They presume the answers to questions are unequivocal.

- They encourage a high degree of guessing, so more items are required; participants can score 50 percent by randomly marking the answers.

Matching Items

Guidelines for constructing matching items are as follows:

1. Place the list of descriptions (the longer list) on the left side of the page so the participant need read it only once. Place the options (the shorter list) on the right to be scanned as

often as needed. An example of a properly constructed set of matching questions appears in Figure 16-1.

2. Make both the descriptions and options list homogeneous. It would be inappropriate for Column B in Figure 16-1 to include items from Bloom's taxonomy such as "analysis" or "synthesis."

3. Provide at least three more options than descriptions or permit the use of each option more than once to reduce guessing.

4. Specify in the instructions the basis for matching and how to mark the answer.

5. Make each option plausible to the uninformed.

6. Arrange the options in some logical order, such as chronological, numerical, or alphabetical to save reading time.

7. Allow between five and fifteen options.

8. Number the descriptions and letter the options.

9. Specify in the instructions whether options can be used more than once.

10. Avoid having more than one correct option for each descriptor; in the example in Figure 16-1, item 1 in Column A should have only one option in Column B that is correct.

Advantages of matching questions include the following:

- They are simpler to construct than multiple-choice or true/false questions.

- They are easier to score than completion questions.

- They are effective in measuring terms and definitions, events and dates, problems and solutions, and names of symbols.

- They tend to discourage guessing.

- They permit the efficient use of space when similar types of information are to be tested.

Disadvantages of matching questions include the following:

- They tend to concentrate on more trivial information (such as categories).
- They often emphasize memorization.
- They are difficult to score using commercial answer sheets.

Instructions: Column A provides a list of learning tasks. Indicate which of Gagné's outcomes (Column B) matches the task in Column A by placing the appropriate letter to the left of the number in Column A. You may use the categories in Column B more than once, but each item in Column A has only one right answer.

Column A	*Column B*
_____ 1. Define "sunk costs."	A. Attitude
_____ 2. List the three principles of just-in-time management.	B. Cognitive skill
_____ 3. Calculate the interest rate.	C. Intellectual skill
_____ 4. Classify each step as auxiliary or essential.	D. Motor skill
_____ 5. Weld a connection.	E. Verbal information
_____ 6. Choose to assist customers who appear confused.	
_____ 7. Demonstrate CPR.	
_____ 8. Determine the correct sample size for a lot.	
_____ 9. Work backward on a problem from the goal to the solution.	
_____10. Formulate a strategic plan.	

Figure 16-1. Sample Set of Matching Questions

Completion Items

Guidelines for constructing completion items are as follows:

1. Use only one blank per item. For example, the following is a faulty item:

   The_____ of patent protection is measured by

   _____.

2. Require single-word answers rather than phrases.

3. Use either direct questions or fill-in-the-blank statements, such as "Write the formula used for determining standard deviation."

4. Place the blank near the end of the sentence rather than near the beginning. For example, the following is a faulty item:

   _____ is likely to increase when a test is lengthened.

5. Word items so they have only one correct answer. For example, the following is a faulty item:

   Copyright does not protect _____.

   The answer the instructor wanted in this item is "expressions." However, a great many words could be placed in the blank without being incorrect.

6. Make sure that the word deleted from the sentence is a significant one. For example, the following is a faulty item:

   A customer can be _____ as anyone who is impacted by the development of the product.

   The answer the instructor wanted in this item is "defined." However, "defined" is not significant.

7. Use "a(n)" before a blank to avoid grammatical cues.

8. Structure all answer blanks to be the same length, regardless of the length of the word to be supplied. Blanks that correspond to the length of the word provide an additional clue to the answer.

   Advantages of completion items include the following:

- Completion items are easier to construct than multiple-choice, true/false, or matching items.
- Guessing is eliminated.
- The items take less time for the participant to complete than multiple-choice questions.

Disadvantages of completion items include the following:

- Completion items are difficult to score; often they must be scored by an expert in the subject matter.
- They tend to measure specific facts rather than general understanding.

This chapter reviews the various kinds of objective tests available to HRD professionals for use in measuring verbal information, and to a lesser degree, certain kinds of intellectual skills. The next chapter discusses developing interview measures.

Developing the Interview

Interviews are a primary tool for identifying customer needs and for establishing customer requirements. They can be used to find the extent to which skills, knowledge, and attitudes (SKA) are being used on the job, as well as to identify the constraints participants face in implementation. Interviews can be conducted on a one-to-one basis in person or by telephone. They can be conducted with groups, in person, by telephone conference call, or by teleconference.

The interview is the measurement tool of choice under the following conditions:

1. There is a need to convey interest, concern, and empathy as well as to collect data.

2. The nature of the behavior is such that it is not possible to observe it directly, such as the skill of problem solving.

3. Information is needed about participants' feelings and intentions as well as actions.

4. The action took place sometime in the past so it can no longer be observed.

5. The interviewer is unsure of what information to collect.

6. The interviewer anticipates that the respondent has not given the topic much previous thought.

The advantages and disadvantages to the interview are summarized in Figure 17-1 and are discussed in the following section.

Advantages of Interviews

1. The interview establishes a perspective independent of preconceived notions.
2. The interviewer is the tool or instrument.

Disadvantages of Interviews

1. The interviewer is the tool or instrument.
2. Interviews are more costly than most other alternatives.
3. The data collection period is longer than it is for other methods.

Figure 17-1. Advantages and Disadvantages of Interviews

ADVANTAGES OF INTERVIEWS

Establishes Independent Perspective

Interviewing establishes a perspective that is independent of preconceived notions. The interview allows the respondent to share in the decisions about what is and is not important to discuss. Unintentional uses of skills can be identified; unanticipated needs can be revealed; and unrecognized constraints can be identified. In this regard, interviews provide much richer data than any other type of measurement, including questionnaires.

Interviewer as Tool

In an interview, the interviewer becomes the data-collection tool; there are both advantages and disadvantages to a human being the data-collection tool, thus "interviewer as tool" has been listed under both headings. It is up to the interviewer to structure the collection of data. The major advantage of using the interviewer as the tool is flexibility; the interviewer can explore those topics that appear to be most fruitful and in whatever depth seems most useful.

DISADVANTAGES OF INTERVIEWS

Interviewer as Tool

A major disadvantage of using a human being as a data-gathering tool is that the interviewer has biases that will be reflected in the questions asked, the intonation used, non-verbal behaviors, and so on. The biases of the interviewer cannot be eliminated; however, the effects of the biases can be reduced in two ways. First, interviewers can openly acknowledge their biases in their summaries of the data; thus the reader can take these biases into account. Second, the interviewer can consciously separate the two types of relationships that exist in an interview: rapport and neutrality.

Rapport refers to the person-to-person relationship in an interview. *Neutrality* refers to the interviewer's relationship to the information. To reduce bias, the interviewer attempts to relate to the respondent with warmth and enthusiasm and to relate to the content with objectivity.

Finally, the data are compromised if the interviewer is not skillful or cannot establish rapport. In either case, misleading data may be collected. Selection and training are two techniques to reduce this disadvantage.

Cost

Interviews are the most costly of the techniques to collect usage data. Cost includes (1) the time of the interviewer, (2) the respondent's time away from work tasks, and (3) the lengthy time that is needed for productive data analysis. Telephone interviews and group interviews lower the first two of these costs considerably.

Lengthy Data Collection Period

The length of the period of data collection is a disadvantage because both individuals and organizations change rapidly. If, for example, the interviews are conducted over a two-month period, information from the first interview may not be comparable to that from the final interview. Telephone interviews and group interviews both shorten the data collection time.

TYPES OF INTERVIEWS

Interviews can be classified into three types: structured, semi-structured, and unstructured.

A *structured interview* can be likened to an oral questionnaire. It is formal in nature and respondents are expected to answer and to elaborate on only the questions asked of them. Lincoln and Guba (1985) provide a helpful contrast between the use of structured and unstructured interviews.

> The structured interview is the mode of choice when the interviewer knows what he or she does not know and can therefore frame appropriate questions to find it out, while the unstructured interview is the mode of choice when the interviewer does not know what he or she doesn't know and must therefore rely on the respondent to tell him or her. (p. 259)

Semistructured interviews are guided by a list of questions or issues to be explored. The exact wording of the questions and the particular sequence in which they are asked are influenced by the way the interview proceeds. The semistructured interview employs both open-ended and close-ended questions. It is appropriate to accumulate questions, adding new questions that have originated in a previous interview. In some cases the interviewer may want to backtrack to previous respondents by telephone or in person if an important new question has emerged.

Unstructured interviews are like conversations; they employ mostly open-ended questions. Unstructured interviews are most useful when the interviewer does not know enough to ask relevant questions. The goal of the unstructured interview may be to formulate questions that can be used at a later date in semistructured interviews, structured interviews, or questionnaires.

As a rule of thumb, more structure is needed under the following conditions:

- Several individuals are conducting the interviews (structure provides consistency across interviewers);
- The interviewer is inexperienced; or
- The questions to ask are known.

GUIDELINES FOR INTERVIEWING

General guidelines for interviewing include the following:

- Hold the interview at the respondent's site if privacy considerations make it possible. Supporting documents are more available at the site, as is the opportunity to meet others who can corroborate the respondent's information.
- Allow at least forty-five minutes between interviews to make notes. This spacing also allows time to prolong interviews that are providing particularly pertinent data.
- Move from the general to the specific if responses without restrictions are wanted. Move from the specific to the general if participants have not given the subject much thought.
- As much as possible, avoid questions as to "why" something happened; they are nearly impossible to ask without sounding parental. In addition they often lead to regressions into the personality of the individual that are less helpful. For example, rather than asking why the respondent did not take a particular concern to his or her manager, it would be more

productive to ask, "What prevented you from talking this over with your manager?"

- The interviewer needs to be aware of three kinds of tension that the respondent may experience at the beginning of the interview (Zemke and Kramlinger, 1988). The tensions are related to the following:

  1. *Intent.* "What is the real reason for this person's interviewing me?"

  2. *Competence.* "Does the interviewer understand this business well enough for us to have a useful discussion?"

  3. *Propriety.* "What relationship do we have with each other? Equals? One-down?"

- Guidelines for how many interviews to schedule does not depend on sampling numbers. Rather the interviews should continue until additional interviews produce only small increments of new information.

- Respondents are not identified on a random basis as might be the case with questionnaires. Randomness is only useful if the data are intended to be representative of all others in that particular population. The purpose of interviews is to obtain an in-depth understanding from a small group of particularly knowledgeable individuals. Therefore, respondents are selected on the basis of their ability to contribute to the understanding. Often a useful source of names is to ask respondents for referrals.

STEPS IN THE INTERVIEW PROCESS

Preparing for the Interview

When preparing for the interview, important steps include the following:

- Review the objectives of the learning event.

- Formulate the specific questions for a structured interview; prepare a list of topics and issues for a semistructured interview.

- Plan how the data will be analyzed; the plan may reveal categorization data that should be collected during the interview, such as the levels of experience of the respondents.

- Determine what demographic information to collect.

- Conduct one or two initial interviews to field test the questions and to become familiar with the respondents' language.

- Revise the interview accordingly.

Conducting the Interview

Steps to follow when conducting the interview are listed as follows:

1. Introduction.

    - State the purpose of the interview.
    - Provide assurances of confidentiality if appropriate.
    - Indicate the approximate length of time the interview will take.
    - Establish rapport with the respondent.
    - Ask permission if tape recording will be used.

2. Ask demographic questions (if needed).

3. Ask interview questions (see Figure 17-2).

    - Probe to elicit additional information.

4. Close the interview.

    - Ask "What have I not asked that I should have asked?"
    - Summarize the major points the respondent made to serve as a validity check.

- Ask for permission to come back for additional questions if needed.

Following the Interview

Following the interview, the interviewer needs to make thorough notes on the interview, recalling as much information verbatim as possible, as well as any general impressions that resulted.

---

1. To what extent have you used _____ [a specific skill]? (The skill, knowledge, or attitude can be drawn from the objectives of the learning event.) Alternatively, if the objectives are not useful in formulating questions, ask "What were the important lessons for you in the learning event?"

2. In what situations have you used that SKA?

  a. Describe an example.

  b. How many times have you used that SKA, or with what frequency?

3. What resulted from using the SKA?

  a. What amounts were involved (dollars, time savings, and so on)?

  b. Who else could I talk to who would support the results?

  c. What records support the results?

4. In what ways had you hoped to use that SKA and were unable to accomplish?

  a. What made using the SKA difficult?

  b. How did you (try to) overcome that difficulty?

  c. What could have happened in the learning event that would have better prepared you to perform the SKA? To overcome the constraint? (Repeat the preceding questions for each of the SKA's involved.)

5. What did you learn that we have not talked about? (Unintentional learning)

**Figure 17-2. Questions for a Semistructured Interview
to Collect Usage Data**

RECORDING THE DATA

Taking notes is the most useful recording technique. A functional process is for the interviewer to make "cueing notes" during the interview and then use the time immediately following the interview to fill out the notes from memory. It is acceptable in an interview to occasionally ask the respondent to pause while the interviewer notes something of importance as in, "That was an important point; give me a moment to get that down." It is also useful to tape record the interview if the interviewer is confident that recording will not inhibit the respondent. Usually people will not object to being recorded; however, if the respondent is offering information critical of the organization or of someone in a position of authority, he or she may be uncomfortable having his or her actual words on tape.

Sometimes a respondent will initially give permission to record the interview on tape and then, some time into the interview, ask that the tape be turned off for a moment in order to relate a specific piece of information. If this happens the interviewer should turn off the tape recorder and place it where the respondent can see that it is off. It is usually not a good idea to turn the recorder on again in that particular interview, even after the respondent has moved to a different subject. The respondent may be reluctant to ask that it be turned off a second time, yet feel uncomfortable about being open.

Even if the respondent does not ask for the tape recorder to be turned off at some point in the interview, the interviewer should watch for nonverbal signs to see how comfortable the respondent is about being taped. For example, if the respondent glances frequently at the recorder, the interviewer may decide it is appropriate to simply reach over and turn the tape off and continue with taking notes.

When an interview is taped it is still useful to take notes. It is time consuming and frustrating to try to find specific passages on a tape without the benefit of accompanying notes. The only situation in which notes are not needed is when the tape is going to be transcribed verbatim, a costly process. In most cases, transcribing takes about three times as long as the interview itself. A transcript, however, does provide the best data for in-depth analysis.

An alternative to a verbatim transcript suggested by Merriam (1988) is the interview log.

> The researcher begins by identifying at the top of a legal-sized pad the name, date, and other necessary details of the interview. The interviewer/researcher then plays the tape and takes notes on important statements or ideas expressed by the informant. Words or phrases or entire sentences are quoted exactly. These notes are coded to the tape counter so the exact location of such words can be accessed quickly at a later time. Tape position is recorded to the left of the words or phrases the researcher deems important. In a column to the far right is space for the researcher to add his or her own observations about what was said. The data on the interview log can later be coded according to the emerging themes or categories for the data analysis phase of the study. (p. 84)

Figure 17-3 illustrates the interview log.

DATA ANALYSIS

Data analysis is the process of making sense out of the data, which involves several steps.

1. Read through the data several times, including the supporting documentation.
2. Identify topics, patterns, or themes based on frequency, borrowed from the literature, or based on the interviewer's own hunches.
3. Use the themes to search for additional data.
4. Organize the information on the basis of the themes as follows:
   - Cutting and pasting duplicated copies of the data;
   - Placing individual data bits on index cards and sorting the cards;

- Developing a coding system to use in the margin; and/or
- Utilizing the search capability of computer word-processing programs or specialized software such as *ETHNOGRAPH* (Seidel & Clark, 1984) or *LISPQUAL* (Druss, 1980).

5. Formulate conclusions based on the categories.

Tape Position	Respondent's Comments	Researcher's Notes
074	Agrees tried to carry out three-part mission	——
093	"Very few," but some top-quality programs; learning centers, persons, finances	*Importance of people and financing in establishment of programs*
109	Describes learning centers; "still have them"—"a real plus"	*Some programs continue despite end of consortium*
117	——	*Consortium as catalyst*
125	Ideas "too grandiose," "spent too much money," "no real funding base"	*Funding is a crucial problem*
134	"Production" focus	——
144	Funding as well as leadership reasons for termination; "he tried to turn it into a competing institution"	*Leadership important—can't become a "competing institution"*
169	Change in focus created problem	*Importance of individual administrator*
179	Leadership problem: "you have to know how to work with people"; must consider member institutions	*Leadership qualities needed in consortium*

Figure 17-3. Sample Interview Log[6]

---

[6]From Merriam, S.B. *Case Study Research in Education: A Qualitative Approach*. San Francisco: Jossey-Bass, 1988, pp. 84-85. Used with permission of publisher.

Questionnaires/Surveys

This chapter continues an in-depth look at various measurement tools by focusing on questionnaires and surveys. Questionnaires and surveys are appropriate when (1) information is needed from a large number of respondents, (2) anonymity is necessary, or (3) numerical data are preferred.

The term *questionnaire* is used here to mean any self-administered measure formulated as dichotomous questions, short-answer questions, rating scales, checklists, ordered scales, semantic differentials, or rank ordering. The advantages and disadvantages of questionnaires are listed briefly in Figure 18-1 and are discussed more fully in the sections that follow.

ADVANTAGES

Anonymity

One of the advantages of questionnaires is that they provide a level of anonymity that no other technique allows. This can encourage individuals to answer questions they might otherwise not answer

Advantages

- Anonymity may allow for more forthright responses.
- Questionnaires can be administered simultaneously.
- Each participant responds to exactly the same questions.
- Data are more easily analyzed than interview data.
- Questionnaires are less costly than most other forms of data collection.
- Evaluators can contact a larger number of participants.

Disadvantages

- Anonymity prevents correlation with premeasures and postmeasures.
- Anonymity may allow unsupported accusations.
- Return rate is often poor, leading to response bias.
- Questionnaires lack the flexibility of interviews.
- Questionnaires disallow correction of the misinterpretation of questions.
- Good reading and writing skills are needed to respond.
- Participant responses are limited to preconceived categories and questions.

Figure 18-1. Advantages and Disadvantages of Questionnaires

for fear of retribution. Anonymity has both advantages and disadvantages, and thus it appears on both lists.

Simultaneous Administration

A second advantage of questionnaires is that they can be administered simultaneously or within a few days of each other. Interviews, observations, and anecdotal records are often spaced over weeks. During the time lag, factors within the organization can alter the way participants respond. Changes within the individual also can occur that impact the response; for example, skills may degrade through disuse or improve as a result of practice.

Consistency in the Questions Asked

Questionnaires ask the same questions of each participant. In interviews, differing emphases in words or tone may change the meaning of the question and the response of the participant.

Easier Data Analysis

Questionnaire data, as well as observation data, are more easily analyzed than interview or anecdotal data. Frequencies, percentages, and measures of central tendency can be calculated and charts and graphs can display the results in easily understood formats.

Lower Cost

Questionnaires are one of the least expensive methods of collecting usage data. As noted in Chapter 8, the average cost is ten dollars per person, considerably less than the thirty or forty dollars per person cost of interviews. Anecdotal records are also lower in cost, but the data analysis can be time consuming and therefore costly. Using existing records is the least costly of the data collection techniques.

Large Numbers of Respondents

One of the most compelling reasons for using questionnaires is the number of respondents who can provide data. No other technique allows the evaluator to obtain information from such a large number of participants.

DISADVANTAGES

Anonymity

The anonymity of questionnaires is, in the author's opinion, a considerably overrated advantage. It disallows correlating the questionnaire with data collected before the learning event, such as demographics or baseline measures. It also prevents comparisons with postmeasures such as performance demonstrations.

The second concern with anonymity is ideological in nature. Anonymous questionnaires allow disgruntled individuals to "get back" at those with whom they are angry without being held responsible for their responses. The idea, for example, that an employee could make detrimental statements about a manager without the manager's even knowing the identity of the accuser, much less having the right to openly confront him or her, seems undemocratic. At the least, anonymity may encourage unsupported accusations.

Poor Return Rate

The return rate of mailed surveys is low, usually 30 to 40 percent. With a low return rate, the sample is likely to be biased. For example, a disproportionate number of those who made extensive use of the skills may have returned the form. When the intent is to determine how a total group responds to an issue, a poor return rate may invalidate the results because of sample bias.

When geographic constraints permit, group administration can substantially increase the return rate. Group administration has the added advantage of allowing the administrator to explain the questionnaire and to respond to questions from respondents.

Lack of Flexibility

A major disadvantage of questionnaires is lack of flexibility. Respondents can answer only the questions addressed to them on the form. If respondents feel other issues are important, they have no way to communicate them. Even when respondents write in comments next to their answers, the analysis is seldom affected in a significant way.

Potential for Misinterpretation

Related to the lack of flexibility is the disadvantage that each person takes a slightly different meaning from a question or statement and responds to it out of that meaning. With questionnaires, there is no way to know exactly what meaning the respondent derived and no way to alter an incorrect interpretation.

In more flexible processes, such as interviews or the use of anecdotes, an evaluator would be better able to identify and to correct misinterpretations.

Need for Good Reading and Writing Skills

In an age of increased illiteracy, as HRD professionals encounter more employees with limited English-proficiency, this disadvantage must be given serious consideration. Respondents often mark a questionnaire even if they cannot read it, preferring that to acknowledging their handicaps. Such responses can invalidate the results. To offset the problem, developers often write questionnaires at fifth-grade or sixth-grade reading levels; however, this does not help non-English speakers or the many who are illiterate. Anecdotal records and observations can also be affected by lack of writing skills; only interviews and the use of existing records are free from this disadvantage.

Questionnaires are most useful when the evaluator thoroughly understands the issues and constructs specific and targeted questions. Questionnaires are less appropriate if the evaluator is on a "fishing expedition"—that is, asking general questions to get an understanding of the issue. Group or individual interviews are a better way to gain understanding. The greatest misuse of question-naires probably comes from not understanding the issues well enough to formulate targeted questions.

Two decision trees for selecting data collection techniques have been provided in this book, one for intellectual skills and one for attitudes. In neither decision tree were surveys a preferred technique; in both decision trees, surveys appear near the bottoms of the lists. A good rule of thumb is to avoid questionnaires if at all possible; they are a last-resort measure.

STEPS IN THE PROCESS OF CREATING QUESTIONNAIRES

In those situations best served by a questionnaire, developers will want to create an instrument that will provide meaningful results to internal and external customers. The twelve-step process set out

1. Interview a sample of the target population.
2. List the variables to be included in the questionnaire.
3. Review variables with stakeholders.
4. Frame the questions.
5. Determine how the data will be analyzed.
6. Try out the questions on a few individuals and revise.
7. Draft the layout and instructions; plan the administrative process.
8. Review the questionnaire and process with stakeholders.
9. Field test the questionnaire and the administrative process.
10. Review the results of the field test.
11. Revise the administrative process, the questionnaire items, and the data analysis process.
12. Review the revised instrument and process with stakeholders.

Figure 18-2. Steps in the Development of Questionnaires

in Figure 18-2 is meant to guide developers to create such an instrument.

1. Interview a sample of the target population. The first step in creating a questionnaire is to interview a sample of participants from the target population. The major purpose of the interview is to determine what issues should be dealt with in the questionnaire. The less familiar the developer is with the issues involved, the greater the number of interviews that should be conducted. A questionnaire can find out "how many," "how intense," or "whether or not," but it is less suited to determining "what." The technique for revealing the "what" is interviews.

A second reason for conducting interviews early in the process is to identify words and phrases representative of the target population that can be used in formulating the questions.

2. List the variables to be included in the questionnaire. The second step in the process is to list the variables to be measured. Despite the temptation to start writing questions at this point, the list of variables provides a reference point to eliminate superfluous questions, the bane of questionnaires. If the developer turns too quickly to writing the questionnaire items, he or she can get tied up in that writing. It is better first to consider the broader issues of which variables to measure and what format is most appropriate.

3. Review variables with stakeholders. Before the questions are framed it is important to review the list of variables with the stakeholders. As noted in Chapter 2, those include both internal and external customers: line managers, participants, instructors, HRD management, and others.

4. Frame the questions. The fourth step is to frame the questions. The format (for example, rating scales, checklists, and so on) for each question should be determined by what is to be measured; it is not necessary for all questions in the document to use the same format. Conway (1988, p.42) makes the following suggestions for determining format:

If the Question is Intended to	Use this Format
• Obtain factual information	Binary
• Distinguish clearly polarized positions	Binary
• Force a choice	Binary
• Measure how a person feels about a number of things in relation to each other	Ranking
• Measure attitude intensity	Rating
• Measure presence or absence of phenomenon	Checklist

5. Determine how the data will be analyzed. The fifth step is to plan the data analysis. Addressing the analysis at this early point is helpful because it may reveal additional items needed for the analysis or point out redundant items. In particular, the data analysis plan helps to highlight the way the data will be categorized, which may indicate the need for additional demographic data. For example, to compare how participants from different shifts respond to a question, the developer would need to add an item that asks participants to identify their shifts.

6. Try out the questions on a few individuals and revise. The sixth step is to try out the questionnaire on a one-to-one basis with several individuals. It is helpful to have each person read and think out loud while answering the questions to pinpoint any confusions or ambivalent items. At this stage, respondents also are able to suggest missing questions or additional responses to be added to checklists. The questionnaire then is revised on the basis of this feedback.

7. Draft the layout and instructions; plan the administrative process. The seventh step is to compose the questionnaire so that it looks exactly the way it will look when it is administered.

Instructions for completing the questionnaire should be drafted and included. If a cover letter is to be used, it also should be prepared. Directions for returning the questionnaire should be planned and included on the form. The process for administration should be planned at this point as well.

8. Review the questionnaire and process with stakeholders. Again the review with stakeholders allows input from those who will be impacted by the questionnaire or the results. These stakeholders may see roadblocks or ways to improve the process that the evaluator had not considered.

9. Field test the questionnaire and the administrative process. The ninth step is to field test the entire system: questionnaire, instructions, and administrative process. The field test should involve a small sample of the population in exactly the same manner that the final questionnaire will be administered.

10. Review the results of the field test. The tenth step is to review the results of the field test. It is helpful to interview several respondents to identify problems that do not show up in the data. Using the data both from the administration and the interviews, review each element as follows:

- Items: review for clarity, additional items, missing alternatives, or confusions in meaning;

- Instructions: review for clarity and completeness;

- Layout: review for length, white space, and professional appearance;

- Cover letter: review for clarity and tone;

- Administrative process: review for ease and efficiency; and

- Data analysis process: review for missing data and appropriate statistical measures.

11. Revise the administrative process, the questionnaire items, and the data analysis process. The eleventh step is the revision of each of the elements: items, instructions, layout, cover letter, administrative process, and data analysis.

12. Review the revised instrument and process with stakeholders. The final step is to review the revised instrument and process with the stakeholders. The purpose of the final review is to ensure that the data collected in the field test will be meaningful to the internal and external customers.

WRITING QUESTIONNAIRE ITEMS

Writing questionnaire items is a difficult task that can look deceptively easy. Every questionnaire has to go through several iterations to eliminate all poorly worded or confusing items. Figure 18-3 lists recommendations for writing questionnaire items; the sections that follow list examples of faulty items and common mistakes.

---

1. Relate each question to only one idea.

2. Avoid words that are inciting or heavily value laden.

3. Avoid negative questions.

4. Provide a way for the respondent to indicate that he or she doesn't know the answer.

5. Italicize or underline key words in the item.

6. Indicate what to do with completed questionnaires; place the address in an obvious place.

7. Use complete sentences for clarity rather than relying on brief or incomplete wording.

8. Make sure the question is one respondents have the information to answer.

9. Make the question specific.

10. Avoid questions that are biased or loaded in one direction.

11. Avoid using qualifiers in both the stem and the responses.

Figure 18-3. Recommendations for Writing Questionnaire Items

1. Relate each question to only one idea. The following is an example of a faulty item:

"How many groups in your department have met and successfully solved problems?"

"Met" and "successfully solved problems" are two different criteria. The respondent may be in doubt as to whether the question is "How many groups have met?" or "How many of the groups that met were successful in solving problems?"

A better wording might be as follows:

"How many groups in your department have met at least once for the purpose of solving a quality related problem?"

"Of those that have met, how many have actually implemented a solution that resulted from the problem solving process?"

2. Avoid words that are inciting or heavily value laden.
The following is an example of a faulty item:

"How many independent contributors in your division have *refused* to use the new forms?"

Words such as "refuse," "deny," and "lazy" may cause a backlash to the question that produces biased results. "Never" and "always" should be avoided for the same reason.

A better wording might be as follows:

"What percentage of independent contributors in your division have begun using the new form?"

3. Avoid negative questions. The following is an example of a faulty item:

"Would you prefer that the implementation not begin before April 17?" Yes ____ No ____

Sentences that include negatives take longer for the respondent to comprehend and are more often misinterpreted. For this reason negatives should be eliminated if at all possible. If it must be included, the negative should be underlined to call the attention of the reader to the word.

A better wording might be as follows:

"Would you prefer the implementation begin after April 17?"

4. *Provide a way for the respondent to indicate that he or she doesn't know the answer.* The following is an example of a faulty item:

"Check each of the waste-reduction activities that have been implemented in your area:"

___ Setup reduction ___ QC inspection ___ Transportation

An empty blank leaves open to interpretation whether the respondent simply did not know or if, in fact, the waste reduction activity had not yet occurred.

The item could be improved by adding a "don't know" option, as follows:

"Check each waste-reduction activity that has been implemented in your area. If you do not know whether one has been implemented, place a check in the 'Don't Know' box."

	Yes	Don't Know
Setup reduction	___	___
QC inspection	___	___
Transportation	___	___

5. *Italicize or underline key words in the item.* The following is an example of a well-constructed item:

"Are you <u>currently</u> involved in a task force?" ___Yes ___No

The intent of the question is to ask about current involvement, not past or future. Underlining adds clarity to the question.

6. *Indicate what to do with completed questionnaires; place the address in an obvious place.* The following is a good example:

"When you have completed the questionnaire, place it in the blue box located at the rear exit of the room."

It is helpful to write the address or return instructions in two places, the beginning and the end. If questionnaires are to be returned by mail, a phone number is also helpful in case a respondent wants to call about a delay or has a question.

7. Use complete sentences for clarity rather than relying on brief or incomplete wording. The following is an example of a faulty item:

"Name_____Department_____Shift_____"

The respondent may be unclear about what response is wanted to the word *Shift*. Several interpretations are possible: Is it the shift on which the questionnaire is being administered? The shift on which he or she currently works? The shift he or she was on at the time of the learning event?

A better working query might be as follows:

"Which shift are you working on this week?"_____

8. Make sure the question is one respondents have the information to answer. The following is an example of a faulty item:

"How many times in a week do the departments under your supervision exchange information?"

_____ 0-3 _____ 4-10 _____ 11-20

An important consideration in designing any questionnaire is determining the person most likely to have the information and addressing the questionnaire to him or her. This point was made in Chapter 3 in the discussion of participant reaction forms. In the preceding example, the division head may not know the answer to the question. As a result the division head may (1) guess, (2) contact the departments to ask for an estimate, or (3) collect data to provide an accurate report. The data that the evaluator analyzes may end up being a combination of facts and guesses.

An alternative would be to ask this question of the department heads who may have more accurate information.

9. Make the question specific. The following is an example of a faulty item:

"How many professional journals do you read on a regular basis?"

The terms *read* and *regularly* are confusing. Does *read* imply every article? What about skimming for useful information? Does *regularly* mean never miss an issue? Every month?

A better question might be as follows:

"List the professional journals to which you subscribe."

10. Avoid questions that are biased or loaded in one direction. The following is an example of a faulty item:

"How well do you like using the new data processing system?"

Built into the question is the assumption that the system is liked. A better wording might be as follows:

"How would you rate the new data processing system?"

Easy to Use			Difficult to Use	
1	2	3	4	5

11. Avoid using qualifiers in both the stem and the responses. The following is an example of a faulty item:

"The application process was fairly easy."

Strongly Disagree	Disagree	No Opinion	Agree	Strongly Agree
1	2	3	4	5

The qualifier "fairly" is in the stem and degrees of agreement are in the responses. The item would be improved by eliminating the word "fairly" from the stem. Another alternative would be to place the adjectives "easy" and "difficult" at each end of the five point scale.

IMPROVING THE RESPONSE RATE

As discussed earlier, the response rate for mailed surveys is very low. Considerable research has been conducted, primarily in marketing, to determine what does and does not improve response rates for questionnaires. Figure 18-4 presents a list of factors constructed from reviews that summarized that research literature (Conway, 1988; Yu & Cooper, 1983).

Factors that improved response rate:

- Persistence in follow-up (this outweighed all other factors and was clearly the most important strategy).

- Preliminary notification, usually by telephone, that a survey was being sent.

- Personalization, such as typed envelopes and individualized salutations.

- Monetary reward for returning the survey; the more money offered, the higher the return rate; prepaid rewards yielded higher returns than promises of rewards.

- Nonmonetary premiums.

- Salience of the topic to the respondent, implying that selection of the target population is important.

- Closed versus open questions.

- Foot-in-the-door techniques, such as getting agreement for a simple task first.

- Postage included with the mailing.

- Sponsorship indicated.

- Use of a deadline.

Factors that showed no significant difference:

- Offers to send results to the respondent.

- Appeals stressing social usefulness or "help-the-researcher."

- Use of a cover letter.

- Length (white space is more important than length).

Figure 18-4. Factors that Affect Response Rates

Validity

This chapter deals with questions of the validity of the evaluation. In its broadest sense, *validity* measures the degree to the evaluation gets the true story. Validity is important because critical decisions about HRD are made based on that story: customer needs are identified, learning events are revised, actions are taken to increase usage, and costs/benefits are determined.

Three questions must be answered to ascertain whether or not HRD is getting the true story:

1. Did the data collection tool measure what it was intended to measure?
2. Was the data collection process appropriate?
3. Was the analysis process appropriate?

Each question will be discussed in turn.

DID THE DATA COLLECTION TOOL MEASURE WHAT IT WAS INTENDED TO MEASURE?

Objective Measures

As Figure 19-1 shows, how validity is assured differs for each type of tool. For objective measures, *item analysis* allows the evaluator to analyze item distracters, item discrimination, and item difficulty. Utilizing an appropriate reading level for the participants is also critical to the validity of objective measures. If participants answer incorrectly because of the difficulty in reading the item, the tool has not tested their knowledge, but rather their reading level. Finally, validity is determined by the extent to which the tool measures the objectives, and the extent to which they, in turn, represent the content. The analysis technique for content validity is the *blueprint*. Techniques for determining reading level, computing item analysis, and constructing a blueprint are discussed later in this chapter.

1. Did the data collection tool measure what it was intended to measure?

- *Objective measures:* item analysis; reading level; blueprint
- *Questionnaires:* reading level; questions based on credible sources; field test
- *Observation checklists:* task analysis; expert judgment
- *Interviews:* summary verified with individual respondents; interviewer's bias revealed; steps taken to preserve anonymity (if controversial)
- *Anecdotal records:* instructions clear and complete; steps taken to preserve anonymity (if controversial)

2. Was the data collection process appropriate?

- *Objective measures:* protocol for administering
- *Questionnaires:* size of sample for survey; representation of sample; return rate
- *Observation checklists:* protocol for administering; training of observers; inter-rater reliability
- *Interviews:* training; degree of structure
- *Anecdotal records:* clear instructions to respondents

3. Was the analysis process appropriate?

- Description of process
- Triangulation of data
- Appropriate statistics

Figure 19-1. Questions of Validity

Questionnaires

The validity of questionnaires is also affected by reading level. In addition, the validity of the content is determined by the legitimacy of the source of the questions. It should be possible to tie each question to a credible source such as (1) interviews with participants, (2) objectives of the learning event, (3) issues raised in the literature on the topic, and so on. Finally, validity is determined by the rigor of the field test to which the questionnaire was subjected. Chapter 18 provides many of the questions that should be addressed in examining the validity of the questionnaire.

Observation Checklists

Observation checklists are validated by two means. First, the observation checklist can be based on or verified through a task analysis conducted by competent performance technologists. Second, in situations in which task analysis is not appropriate, the opinion of two or more subject matter experts can be used to validate the product or process checklist. A person is deemed an expert by virtue of his or her credentials, length of experience, or the acknowledgment of peers. Validating the checklist with an expert is necessary even if the individual who constructed the checklist is also an expert in the subject matter.

Interviews

Interviews are validated by the interviewer checking the summary of the respondent's statements directly with the respondent. The intent of this process is not to verify the truthfulness of the respondent's statements, but rather to verify that the interviewer has accurately understood the respondent. A second validating process is to reveal the interviewer's biases in the report of the data. As discussed in Chapter 17, there is no way to eliminate interviewer bias; however, the distortions created by bias can be corrected, to some extent, by allowing the reader to take it into account. Finally, the validity of interviews is aided by providing assurances of confidentiality to respondents that permit them to provide more accurate information than they would otherwise be willing to reveal.

Anecdotal Records

For anecdotal information, validity is assisted by assuring that the instructions to the individuals writing the anecdotes are clear and complete. Examples are helpful in this regard. It is also useful for the evaluator to check the first few anecdotes the individual produces (perhaps during the learning event) to make sure the instructions were understood and are being followed. If the data are of a controversial nature, validity will be assisted by assuring anonymity.

WAS THE DATA COLLECTION PROCESS APPROPRIATE?

Objective Measures

The process for ensuring validity is determined by the type of tool to be used. For objective measures, the validity of the data collection process is ensured by using a protocol for administering the instrument. The protocol assures that all administrations are similar and that the intent of the tool is communicated.

Questionnaires

For questionnaires, the validity of the data collection process is related to the size and representation of the sample. The sample must be large enough to be able to generalize from the results. For the same reasons the representation in the sample must be considered. For example, if the results are to be generalized to all shifts, then each shift must be represented in the sample. And, as discussed in the Chapter 18, the return rate must be adequate and must not discount a specific segment of the population, such as unhappy employees or those who do not read well. A chart of appropriate sample sizes for various populations, taken from Zemke and Kramlinger (1988), is included as Table 19-1 (see page 238).

Observation Checklists

For observation, the validity of the data collection is dependent on the protocol for administering; that is, the same instructions and time limits must be provided to each participant. Second, if the observation tool is a rating scale that requires judgment, training may be needed to complete the scale in accordance with its intent. Finally, if more than one rater is involved, provisions need to be made to ensure inter-rater reliability. This reliability is obtained by raters independently rating the same incident (often from a video-tape) and comparing scores. The process is repeated with various incidents until there is no significant difference in the way raters mark the form for each incident.

Interviews

For interviews, validation of the data collection process is needed when more than one interviewer is involved. When several individuals are going to be conducting interviews, training needs to be provided to ensure that all are interviewing in the same manner, in terms of length of time, amount of probing, initial explanation, and so on. The greater the number of interviewers involved, the more structured the interview needs to be.

Anecdotal Records

Because the data collection process for anecdotal records involves only the individual keeping the record, there are no specific strategies needed—assuming that the initial instructions were clear and complete.

WAS THE ANALYSIS PROCESS APPROPRIATE?

Three validity considerations are important for the analysis process. Particularly with qualitative data such as interviews and anecdotes, the process used to analyze the data needs to be spelled out for the reader. Such information may not go into the final report, but needs to be available at a minimum. Second, data from more than one source improve the validity of the analysis; for example, interview data may be supported by numbers related to the results discussed in the interview; observation of performance may be supported by scores on objective measures that cover supporting theory. This cross-checking is known as *triangulation*. Finally, statistics that are appropriate to the level of data (nominal, ordinal, interval, ratio) and to the size and nature of the sample need to be employed.

ITEM ANALYSIS

Item analysis is a process used to assess the quality of individual items on an objective measure. Several analyses can be conducted on each item. Figure 19-2 displays a sample set of data for twenty-one students on an eight-item multiple choice measure. (Although it is unlikely that an eight-item measure would be long enough to be valid, the limited number of items is used here for simplicity in the illustration.) The scores are arranged from the best score on the measure, Participant 1, to the poorest score, Participant 21. The correct answer to each of the eight items is shown in parentheses beneath the item number.

ANALYSIS OF RESPONSES OF NAIVE LEARNERS

The first analysis is made by administering the measure to a group of individuals who would not be expected to know the material covered by the measure. Because they are naive, the only ways these individuals would be able to select correct answers are (1) if the

Item Numbers and Correct Responses

Parti-cipant	1 (D)	2 (B)	3 (A)	4 (D)	5 (B)	6 (D)	7 (E)	8 (A)	Number of Correct Responses
1	D	B	A	B	B	D	E	A	= 7
2	D	B	A	B	B	D	E	A	= 7
3	D	B	A	B	B	D	E	A	= 7
4	D	B	A	B	B	D	E	A	= 6
5	D	A	A	D	B	D	E	C	= 6
6	D	B	A	B	B	D	E	B	= 6
7	D	B	A	D	C	D	B	C	= 5
8	D	D	A	B	B	D	E	D	= 5
9	D	B	A	E	D	D	D	E	= 4
10	D	B	B	E	B	C	E	B	= 4
11	D	E	A	D	B	B	D	C	= 4
12	D	D	A	B	C	D	E	E	= 4
13	D	B	D	C	E	D	C	B	= 3
14	D	A	E	D	B	E	B	B	= 3
15	D	C	B	D	C	B	C	E	= 2
16	D	E	D	E	C	D	D	C	= 2
17	D	A	C	D	D	B	B	C	= 2
18	D	E	E	E	C	A	D	A	= 2
19	D	C	E	D	C	E	B	B	= 2
20	D	D	B	D	E	B	C	C	= 2
21	C	A	D	D	A	C	B	E	= 1
Total Correct	20	9	10	9	10	12	9	5	
Incorrect Items Selected	ABCDE 001-0	ABCDE 4-233	ABCDE -4133	ABCDE 071-4	ABCDE 1-622	ABCDE 142-2	ABCDE 0534-	ABCDE -5614	

Figure 19-2. Hypothetical Objective Measure Results

answers are common knowledge, (2) if the measure itself provides a clue, or (3) if they make lucky guesses. If the respondents are guessing, one would expect an even distribution of responses across each of the letters as shown: "A," 20 percent; "B," 20 percent; "C," 20 percent; "D," 20 percent; and "E," 20 percent. By administering the measure and then constructing a chart modeled on Figure 19-2, it is possible to analyze the items. For example on question one, twenty of the twenty-one respondents marked the correct answer, "D." The evaluator can assume that either most people already knew the information (an indication that it may not need to be taught or tested) or answers "A," "B," "C," and "E" of the item were so unbelievable that no one chose to mark them (in which case better distracters need to be constructed). As another example of the analysis, none of the respondents marked "A" for item 7. If guessing were occurring, at least four respondents (20 percent) would have selected that distracter. By reviewing item 7, it may be possible to determine what makes that distracter less attractive to the respondents. By analyzing each item in this manner, poor items can be improved or eliminated.

ITEM DIFFICULTY

Item difficulty computes the proportion of the participants who answered the item correctly. It is computed by dividing the number who selected the correct answer by the total number who answered the question.

$$\frac{\text{Item}}{\text{Difficulty}} = \frac{\text{Number who selected the correct answer}}{\text{Total number who answered the item}}$$

If the scores in Figure 19-2 are now considered the results of an objective measure administered at the end of a learning event, item difficulty can be computed with the same set of data.

For example, the item difficulty for item 2 is as follows:

$$\frac{9}{21} = .43 \text{ (moderately difficult)}$$

That number can be compared with the following item difficulty for item 1:

$$\frac{20}{21} = .95 \text{ (easy)}$$

A ratio that indicated difficulty (between .00 and .30) for a postmeasure item could have the following possible meanings:

1. It was poorly taught or not taught at all;

2. The item wording is confusing to respondents; or

3. The item is so difficult that only the most knowledgeable participants were able to answer correctly.

An easy item-difficulty ratio (ranging from 0.80 to 1.00) in a postmeasure could mean the following:

1. The information was well taught;

2. The distracters were unbelievable or the answer was cued in some way; or

3. The participants already knew the information (if this has not already been determined by a test of naive learners).

If several items on the measure are testing the same information (for example, items 3, 6, and 8), and one item is found to be more difficult than the others (for example, .48, .57, and .24 respectively), it would be reasonable to examine the difficult item (8) to determine why participants did less well. The item may be misleading, or it simply may be difficult item.

Item-difficulty ratios point to potential problems, but do not indicate what the problem is or how to fix it. For those answers, the evaluator must rely on logic and reason applied to the tool. Interviewing participants can also provide insight into why an item was marked in a particular way.

ITEM DISCRIMINATION

Item discrimination examines what category of participants answered the item correctly. To compute item discrimination, participants' scores are ordered from highest to lowest as illustrated in Figure 19-2. The group is divided into an upper and lower group. In Figure 19-2, the upper group is made up of Participants 1-10 and the lower group, Participants 12-21. The score for Participant 11 is disregarded to keep the two groups of equal size.

The following formula is used to compute the item discrimination:

$$\frac{\left(\begin{array}{c}\text{Number who got} \\ \text{the item correct} \\ \text{in upper group}\end{array}\right) - \left(\begin{array}{c}\text{Number who got} \\ \text{the item correct} \\ \text{in lower group}\end{array}\right)}{\text{Number of participants in either group}}$$

For example, in item 7, the formula yields the following result:

$$\frac{8 - 1}{10} = .70$$

Applying the formula to item 4 results in the following outcome:

$$\frac{2 - 6}{10} = -.40$$

When item discrimination is computed, three types of scores are possible: *positive* (as in item 7), *negative* (as in item 4), and *zero*. A positive score is preferred, which means that those who did well overall on the measure were more likely to choose the correct answer for this item.

A negative score means those who did poorly overall on the measure were more likely to choose the correct answer for this item. Looking at item 4 in more detail in Figure 19-2, it appears that the upper group tended to choose B as the correct answer. A negative score is an indication that something is wrong with the item. Why would the "best" learners miss this item? Again the evaluator must use logic and reason to ferret out the answer; item discrimination only points to a potential problem.

Although item analysis is most useful for a multiple-choice format, it can also be computed for true/false and completion items.

BLUEPRINT

An objective/item blueprint is a way to determine the extent to which the measure is related to the objectives. The blueprint is created as a matrix with the objectives on one axis and the items on the other. The blueprint in Figure 19-3 makes evident a validity problem with the sample measure. The matrix reveals that Objective 6 is not measured at all and that items 2 and 7 do not appear to be related to any of the objectives for the learning event.

ITEMS

OBJECTIVES	1	2	3	4	5	6	7	8
1	X							
2			X					
3				X				
4					X	X		
5								X
6								

Figure 19-3. An Objective/Item Blueprint

The second validity issue is related to the extent to which the objectives represent the content. Again a matrix can be constructed to examine this question by placing the objectives on one axis and the time frames of the learning event on the other, as shown in Figure 19-4. The length of time (in hours) spent related to each objective is placed in the matrix. This illustration assumes that the learning event is three days in length. The sample content blueprint again reveals some validity issues. For example, Objective 5 does not have any time associated with it. Objective 4 has only .5 hours associated with it, yet the earlier matrix showed Objective 4 to have twice as many questions as any other objective. The evaluator might consider whether the number of items in the measure reflects the level of importance of this objective to the total learning. The matrix also shows that only one hour of Monday afternoon is spent on an objective. The evaluator may want to reassess the agenda to determine what other learning occurring in that time frame should be stated as an objective.

CONTENT EXPRESSED IN HOURS

OBJECTIVES	MONDAY AM	MONDAY PM	TUESDAY AM	TUESDAY PM	WEDNESDAY AM	WEDNESDAY PM
1	.5		2	1		
2	2					4
3		1	1	1	3	
4			.5			
5						
6	.5			2		

Figure 19-4. A Content/Time Frames Blueprint

PROTOCOL FOR ADMINISTRATION

A major concern with using any kind of performance measure is that each participant have the same understanding of what he or she is to do and why. If only one instructor is involved, this concern is lessened; however, if several instructors are administering the same measure, differences in the way instructions are given may result in considerably different scores. This validity is achieved by creating a test protocol to which each instructor or evaluator subscribes. Although each protocol is unique in that it addresses the specific issues of a given measure, guidelines are offered here for developing a protocol.

Guidelines Addressed to the Instructor or Administrator of the Measure

1. Allocate adequate time for administering the measure. Avoid conveying the impression that the measure is an add-on as in, "Don't leave yet, we still have to do the test."

2. If objective measures are employed, it is helpful to have each participant score his or her own measure. Self-scoring runs the risk that someone will change a mark, but that is still generally preferable to asking participants to exchange papers, which implies they will cheat. In part, self-scoring is a time-related issue, in that the instructor attempting to score all measures can delay the final review. That review is important because it increases participants' learning.

3. If participants do mark their own objective measures, explain how to do the scoring (such as "Mark each correct answer with an X to the left of the answer blank; put the total number of right answers in the upper right-hand corner."). Without clear instructions, some participants mark wrong answers and others mark right answers.

4. Review the answers with the participants as they score the measure or immediately after.

5. Collect all copies of the measures before participants leave. This is particularly true for objective measures for which it is possible for participants to simply memorize the correct letter to mark.

6. If the postmeasure is a performance demonstration, review the checklist with each participant immediately following the performance demonstration. Unlike objective measures, it is usually not necessary to retain the checklists for performance demonstrations.

Guidelines on What to Say to Participants About the Performance Measure

1. Indicate early in the learning event (when the objectives are introduced is a good time) both that performance will be measured and what the performance criteria will be. Explain who will see the results and in what form.

2. Avoid sounding apologetic for asking participants to demonstrate that they have learned.

3. Explain the directions verbally even if they are also written; for objective measures it is helpful to walk around the room, observing how participants are marking the answers to be sure they have understood the directions.

4. Suggest the average or approximate amount of time participants will have to work on the measure. In most situations time limits are not critical to performance.

5. Make a statement to the whole group that those with special needs (learning disabilities, difficulty with reading, English-as-a-Second Language, test anxiety, and so on) can arrange an alternative time to complete the measure (when it can be administered orally, with an interpreter, with additional time, and so on).

6. Avoid school language in the explanation of the measure, including such words as "test," "pass/fail," "you get an A,"

and so on. School-related processes also should be avoided, such as seating the participants one chair apart or having participants clear their areas of papers.

SAMPLE SIZE

When using questionnaires or surveys the optimum size is the total group. Asking the questions of everyone is the only way to know for sure how the total group responds to an issue or question. When the total group cannot be reached either because of costs, time, or other constraints, a sample is drawn to represent the total. The critical factor in selecting the sample is that it be drawn in such a way that everyone in the total population has an equal chance of being selected. A common method used to ensure this is to systematically select every "nth" name on a list. Another accepted method is to assign a number to each name and then to use a table of random numbers to guide the selection.

A *stratified sample* is used when the evaluator wants to ensure that individuals from different groups are represented in the sample. An example might be a questionnaire administered to determine the extent of usage of a particular skill that has been taught to line workers who work on three different shifts. It would be important that workers from all shifts be included in the sample, and that they are represented in the sample in approximately the same proportions as in the real population. Sample names would still be drawn randomly, but instead of drawing from a total list, the evaluator would draw the appropriate number of names from lists subdivided for each shift.

The purpose in taking such care about how the sample is drawn is that the evaluator intends to say the findings are true not just of the individuals who completed the questionnaire, but of those who did not as well. It is this concern for being able to generalize to a larger population that necessitates care in selecting the sample. Zemke and Kramlinger (1988) provide a helpful chart (see Table 19-1) based on Hays's *Statistics for the Social Sciences* (1973) to use

Table 19-1. A Sample Size Table for Proportions[7]

Degree of Accuracy = ± .05		Proportion of Sample Size = 0.5		Confidence Level = 95%	
Population	Sample	Population	Sample	Population	Sample
10	9	230	144	1400	301
15	14	240	147	1500	305
20	19	250	151	1600	309
25	23	260	155	1700	313
30	27	270	158	1800	316
35	32	280	162	1900	319
40	36	290	165	2000	322
45	40	300	168	2200	327
50	44	320	174	2400	331
55	48	340	180	2600	334
60	52	360	186	2800	337
65	55	380	191	3000	340
70	59	400	196	3500	346
75	62	420	200	4000	350
80	66	440	205	4500	354
85	69	460	209	5000	356
90	73	480	213	6000	361
95	76	500	217	7000	364
100	79	550	226	8000	366
110	85	600	234	9000	368
120	91	650	241	10000	369
130	97	700	248	15000	374
140	102	750	254	20000	376
150	108	800	259	30000	379
160	113	850	264	40000	380
170	118	900	269	50000	381
180	122	950	273	60000	381
190	127	1000	277	70000	382
200	131	1100	284	120000	382
210	136	1200	291	160000	383
220	140	1300	296	1,000,000	383

This table tells you the number of people you must survey to accurately represent the views of the population under study. Accurate here means reliable at the .005 reliability level. In other words, the chances of the results being funky is 5/100.

[7] R. Zemke/T. Kramlinger, *Figuring Things Out,* © 1982, Addison-Wesley Publishing Co., Inc., Reading, Massachusetts. Reprinted by permission of the publisher.

in selecting sample size. It should be noted that if the population is stratified, the numbers apply to each strata.

As discussed earlier, getting all or nearly all the surveys back is as critical for validity as is the number selected. No matter how much care was taken in selecting the sample, a biased return will prevent the evaluator from being able to generalize the findings to the total population.

READING LEVEL

The reading level of the measure is a critical issue for validity. If the reading level is too difficult for the respondent, the evaluator cannot determine whether incorrect responses were a result of the individual not having gained the skills, knowledge, or attitudes to answer correctly, or whether the respondent simply could not understand the item.

Readability is a function of the number of large words (three syllables or more), the length and complexity of the sentences, and the level of abstraction involved in the meaning. Most formulas rely only on the first two factors to compute the reading level, as the third is difficult to convert to a number. In addition, most formulas for determining reading level were intended to be used with passages of text, not test items. As a result, there is some controversy as to their accuracy when used to judge the reading level of test items (Duncan, 1986), particularly with multiple-choice test items that have multiple endings to a single stem. Given that caveat, an estimate of reading level is still useful.

Software programs are available that automatically compute the reading level of a passage; *RightWriter* (1988) is an example of one such program. It is also possible to compute the scores by hand. The formula for calculating Gunning's (1968) Fog Index is as follows:

$$\text{Reading level} = \left(\frac{\text{Number of words in sentences of a passage}}{\text{Number of sentences in the passage}} + \frac{\text{Number of three-syllable words in the passage}}{} \right) \times .4$$

The following are steps in the process of computing the Gunning Fog Index:

1. Count the number of words in consecutive sentences. Stop the sentence count with the end of the sentence nearest a total of one hundred words.

2. Count the number of sentences in the same passage.

3. Divide the total number of words in the passage (step 1) by the number of sentences (step 2). This gives the average sentence length of the passage.

4. Count the number of words in the passage that have three or more syllables. Do not count names, combinations of short easy words like "bookkeeper," or verb forms that become three syllables long by the addition of the suffixes "-ed" or "-es," such as "created" or "trespasses."

5. Add the number of words with three or more syllables (step 4) to the average computed in step 3.

6. Multiply the sum of step 5 by .4 to get the reading level.

An acceptable reading level depends on the level of education of the participants. Newspapers are generally kept below sixth grade level. Gunning (1968) feels all clear communication can and should be written at or below a reading level of twelfth grade.

If the reading level of the test items is too high, the sentences can be shortened and the three-syllable words replaced with simpler words. Duncan (1986) cautions against shortening the sentences by taking out important clauses, preferring that the clauses be made into independent sentences, even at the risk of seeming redundant.

Appendix

**INSTRUCTOR BEHAVIORS AND COURSE DESIGN
OBSERVATION FORM**

Course Name_____ # _____ Module # _____

Organization_____ Location _____

Instructor_____ Length of course _____

Evaluator_____ Date reviewed _____

Instructions: Some items ask you to consider the actions of the instructor over the entire observation period; those items are scaled. For other items, only a check mark is needed if the action occurred. If you did not have an opportunity to observe the action, place a check in the "No opportunity to observe" blank. The comments line is the most important response; please use it freely.

I. INTRODUCTION

	No opportunity to observe	*Yes*
A. Introduced self	_____	_____

Comments_____

B. Introduced participants

	No opportunity to observe	*Yes*
1. Expressed interest in participants	_____	_____

Comments_____

	Authority			Collaborator
2. Established self as:	1 2 3 4 5			

Comments_____

C. Introduction of the course

	No opportunity to observe	Yes
1. Communicated agenda/logistics	_____	_____

Comments_____

	No opportunity to observe	Yes
2. PROVIDED COURSE OVERVIEW	_____	_____

Comments_____

	No opportunity to observe	Yes
3. COMMUNICATED COURSE OBJECTIVES	_____	_____

Comments_____

	No opportunity to observe	Yes
4. MODULE OBJECTIVES ARE MEASURABLE	_____	_____

Comments_____

	Rarely			Consistently
5. COMMUNICATED MODULE OBJECTIVES	1 2 3 4 5			

Comments_____

Instructions: Sections II through VII each apply to a different method of instruction. Each is marked only if that type of instruction was employed.

II. LECTURE

A. Teaching technique

	Unorganized		Organized
1. Presentation	1 2 3	4 5

Comments_____

	Rarely	Consistently
2. Reminded participants of related knowledge	1 2 3	4 5

Comments_____

	Rarely	Consistently
3. Used variety of examples for concepts	1 2 3	4 5

Comments_____

B. Style

	Unacceptable	Acceptable
1. Style of presentation for this audience	1 2 3	4 5

Comments_____

	Rarely	Consistently
2. Sought feedback on participant understanding	1 2 3	4 5

Comments_____

	Too slow	Too fast
3. Pacing appropriate for the density	1 2 3	4 5

Comments_____

	Easily got off topic	Stayed focused
4. Stayed on topic	1 2 3	4 5

Comments_____

C. Knowledge of subject matter

	Little knowledge			Extensive knowledge	
1. Instructor answers displayed:	1	2	3	4	5

Comments_____

	Uncertain			Confident	
2. Related to material, instructor appeared:	1	2	3	4	5

Comments_____

III. LEADING A DISCUSSION

	Rarely			Consistently	
A. Asked open-ended questions	1	2	3	4	5

Comments_____

	Rarely			Consistently	
B. Refrained from responding to all comments	1	2	3	4	5

Comments_____

	Rarely			Consistently	
C. Prevented a few from dominating	1	2	3	4	5

Comments_____

	Rarely			Consistently	
D. Kept discussion on topic	1	2	3	4	5

Comments_____

IV. EXPERIENTIAL ACTIVITIES

	No opportunity to observe	*Yes*
A. Stated purpose/outcome of activity	_____	_____

Comments_____

	Confusing				*Clear*
B. Instructions were:	1	2	3	4	5

Comments_____

C. Debriefed activity

	No opportunity to observe	*Yes*
1. Discussed feelings and reactions	_____	_____

Comments_____

	No opportunity to observe	*Yes*
2. Sought patterns in the data	_____	_____

Comments_____

	No opportunity to observe	*Yes*
3. Helped group reach generalizations	_____	_____

Comments_____

	No opportunity to observe	*Yes*
4. Helped group explore ways to apply findings	_____	_____

Comments_____

V. SKILL PRACTICE

A. Management of the skill practice

	No opportunity to observe	*Yes*
1. Stated purpose of the skill practice	_____	_____

Comments_____

	Confusing			*Clear*	
2. Instructions were:	1	2	3	4	5

Comments_____

	No opportunity to observe	*Yes*
3. Provided instructions for peer feedback	_____	_____

Comments_____

	No opportunity to observe	*Yes*
4. Instructor offered appropriate feedback	_____	_____

Comments_____

	No opportunity to observe	*Yes*
5. Debriefed practice	_____	_____

Comments_____

B. Time for practice

	No opportunity to observe	*Yes*
1. ADEQUATE PRACTICE TIME WAS ALLOCATED	_____	_____

Comments_____

2. ADEQUATE NUMBER OF SKILL
   PRACTICES WERE PROVIDED

	No opportunity to observe	Yes
	_____	_____

Comments_____

VI. INSTRUMENTATION

	Confusing			Clear	
A. Instructions were:	1	2	3	4	5

Comments_____

	No opportunity to observe	Yes
B. Explained theory of instrument	_____	_____

Comments_____

	Confusing			Clear	
C. Directions for scoring:	1	2	3	4	5

Comments_____

	No opportunity to observe	Yes
D. Provided adequate interpretation	_____	_____

Comments_____

	No opportunity to observe	Yes
E. Processed the experience	_____	_____

Comments_____

	No opportunity to observe	Yes
F. Avoided defending instrument	_____	_____

Comments_____

VII. CLASSROOM MANAGEMENT

A. Difficult participants

	Discourteous			*Courteous*
1. Handled angry participants with courtesy	1	2	3	4	5

Comments_____

	Defended position			*Open to others*
2. Allowed for differing views	1	2	3	4	5

Comments_____

	Rarely			*Consistently*
3. Prevented domination by a few participants	1	2	3	4	5

Comments_____

	Rarely			*Consistently*
4. Controlled outside conversations	1	2	3	4	5

Comments_____

B. Time

	No opportunity to observe	*Yes*
1. Began on time	_____	_____

Comments_____

	No opportunity to observe	*Yes*
2. Started on time after breaks	_____	_____

Comments_____

	No opportunity to observe	Yes
3. Ended on time	_____	_____

Comments_____

C. Room arrangement

	No opportunity to observe	Yes
1. Arrangement suited to type of instruction	_____	_____

Comments_____

	No opportunity to observe	Yes
2. Size of room appropriate	_____	_____

Comments_____

VIII. MEDIA

A. Introduction

	No opportunity to observe	Yes
1. Explained objective of media	_____	_____

Comments_____

	No opportunity to observe	Yes
2. Suggested what to watch for	_____	_____

Comments_____

B. Quality

	Unprofessional/Professional
1. PROFESSIONAL QUALITY	1 2 3 4 5

Comments_____

	No opportunity to observe	Yes
2. CURRENT KNOWLEDGE	_____	_____

Comments_____

	No opportunity to observe	Yes
3. SATISFIES EEO REGULATIONS	_____	_____

Comments_____

	No opportunity to observe	Yes
C. Debriefed media	_____	_____

Comments_____

IX. CONCLUSION OF COURSE

	No opportunity to observe	Yes
A. Instructor summarized what had been taught	_____	_____

Comments_____

	No opportunity to observe	Yes
B. PARTICIPANTS CONSTRUCTED AN ACTION PLAN	_____	_____

Comments_____

	No opportunity to observe	Yes
C. Follow-up was established	_____	_____

Comments_____

X. EVALUATION

	No opportunity to observe	Yes
A. POSTTEST APPROPRIATE FOR OUTCOMES	_____	_____

Comments_____

	No opportunity to observe	Yes
B. POSTTEST EVALUATED STATED OBJECTIVES	_____	_____

Comments_____

	No opportunity to observe	Yes
C. All objectives covered in the course	_____	_____

Comments_____

XI. PARTICIPANT MATERIALS

	No opportunity to observe	Yes
A. ADEQUATE GLOSSARY	_____	_____

Comments_____

	No opportunity to observe	Yes
B. ADEQUATE BIBLIOGRAPHY	_____	_____

Comments_____

	No opportunity to observe	Yes
C. NECESSARY PERFORMANCE AIDS PROVIDED	_____	_____

Comments_____

	Difficult to locate			Easy to locate	
D. ORGANIZED FOR EASE IN LOCATING ITEMS	1	2	3	4	5

Comments_____

	No opportunity to observe	Yes
E. APPROPRIATE READING LEVEL	_____	_____

Comments_____

XII. INSTRUCTOR MATERIALS

Instructor's materials contain:

	Yes	No
1. Description of target population	_____	_____
2. Participant prerequisites	_____	_____
3. Recommended minimum and maximum numbers of participants	_____	_____
4. Suggested instructor qualifications	_____	_____
5. Recommended length of learning event	_____	_____
6. Recommended spacing and timing of modules	_____	_____
7. Facilities requirements	_____	_____
8. Equipment needs	_____	_____
9. List of participant materials	_____	_____
10. List of instructor materials	_____	_____
11. Evaluation design		
Suggested protocol	_____	_____
Instruments for end of learning event	_____	_____
Instruments for measuring on-the-job behaviors	_____	_____
Evidence of validation of instruments/norms	_____	_____

	Yes	No
Scoring keys/suggested answers	_____	_____
Minimum criteria suggested	_____	_____
12. Supporting readings	_____	_____
13. References for further reading	_____	_____

Bibliography

Argyris, C. (1985). *Strategy, change and defensive routines.* Boston, MA: Pitman.

Argyris, C., Putnam, R., & Smith, D.M. (1985). *Action science.* San Francisco: Jossey-Bass.

Borich, G.D. (1980). A needs assessment model for conducting follow-up studies. *Journal of Teacher Education, 31* (3), 39-41.

Bowen, D.E., & Jones, G.R. (1986). Transaction cost analysis of service organization-customer exchange. *Academy of Management Review, 11* (2), 428-441

Bowen, D.E., Siehl, C., & Schneider, B. (1989). A framework for analyzing customer service orientations in manufacturing. *Academy of Management Review, 14* (1), 75-95.

Brandenburg, D.C., & Schultz, E. (1988, April). *The status of training evaluation: An update.* Presentation at the National Society of Performance and Instruction Conference, Washington, DC.

Brinkerhoff, R.O. (1983). The success case: A low-cost, high-yield evaluation. *Training and Development Journal, 37* (8), 58-61.

Brinkerhoff, R.O. (1987). *Achieving results from training: How to evaluate human resource development to strengthen programs and increase impact.* San Francisco: Jossey-Bass.

Brush, D.H., & Licata, B.J. (1983). The impact of skill learnability on the effectiveness of managerial training and development. *Journal of Management, 9* (1), 27-39.

Bunker, K.A., & Cohen, S.L. (1977). The rigors of training evaluation: A discussion and field demonstration. *Personnel Psychology, 30,* 525-541.

Campbell, J.P. (1971). Personnel training and development. *Annual Review of Psychology, 22,* 565-602.

Campbell, J., Dunnette, M., Lawler, E., & Weick, K. (1970). *Managerial behavior, performance and effectiveness.* New York: McGraw-Hill.

Casner-Lotto & Associates. (1988). *Successful training strategies.* San Francisco: Jossey-Bass.

Castle, D.K. (1989, May/June). Management design: A competency approach to create exemplary performers. *Performance and Instruction,* pp. 42-48.

Clement, R.W. (1981, Winter). Evaluating the effectiveness of management training: Progress during the 1970s and prospects for the 1980s. *Human Resource Management,* pp. 8-13.

Clement, R.W. (1982). Testing the hierarchy theory of training evaluation: An expanded role for trainee reactions. *Public Personnel Management Journal, 11* (2), 176-184.

Conway, M.J. (1988, April). *Improving questionnaire response rates: Empirical and practical guidelines.* Presented at 1988 Annual Conference: National Society for Performance and Instruction, Washington, DC.

Crown Copyright Reserved. (1977). *Army Code No. 70670. Job Analysis for Training. Pamphlet No. 2.* United Kingdom.

Dick, W. (1986). The function of the pretest in the instructional design process. *Performance and Instruction, 25* (4), 6-7.

Dixon, N.M. (1987). Meet training's goals without reaction forms. *Personnel Journal, 66* (8), 108-115.

Dixon, N.M. (1989). Self-defeating strategies of training departments. *Performance and Instruction, 28* (7), 23-26.

Dixon, N.M. (1990). The relationship between training responses on participant reaction forms and posttest scores. *Human Resource Development Quarterly, 1* (2), 129-137.

Druss, K.A. (1980). The analysis of qualitative data: A computer program. *Urban Life, 9,* 332-353.

Duncan, R.E. (1986). *Theoretically based test item readability: An approach to estimating the degree to which an item can be understood and answered correctly.* Unpublished doctoral dissertation, University of Texas, Austin, TX.

Fowler, F.J. (1984). *Survey research methods.* Newbury Park, CA: Sage.

Gagné, E.D. (1985). *The cognitive psychology of school learning.* Boston, MA: Little, Brown.

Gagné, R.M., & Briggs, L.J. (1979). *Principles of instructional design.* New York: Holt, Rinehart and Winston.

Georgenson, D.L. (1982). The problem of transfer calls for partnership. *Training and Development Journal, 36* (10), 75-78.

Gilbert, T. (1978). *Human competence.* New York: McGraw-Hill.

Goldstein, I.L. (1980). Training in work organizations. *Annual Review of Psychology, 31,* 229-273.

Gronlund, N.E. (1988). *How to construct achievement tests* (4th ed.). Englewood Cliffs, NJ: Prentice-Hall.

Gunning, R. (1968). *The technique of clear writing.* New York: McGraw-Hill.

Hagman, J.D. (1980). *Effects of training task repetition on retention and transfer of maintenance skills* (Research Report 1271). Alexandria, VA: U.S. Army Research Institute.

Harmon, P. (1984). A hierarchy of performance variables. *Performance and Instruction, 23* (10), 27-28.

Hays, W.L. (1973). *Statistics for the social sciences* (2nd ed.). New York: Holt, Rinehart and Winston.

Head, G.E., & Buchannan, C.C. (1981). Cost/benefit analysis of training: A foundation for change. *NSPI Journal, 20* (10), 25-27.

Henerson, M.E., Morris, L.L., & Fitz-Gibbon, C.T. (1978). *How to measure attitudes.* Newbury Park, CA: Sage.

House, R.F. (1968). Leadership training: Some dysfunctional consequences. *Administrative Science Quarterly, 12* (4), 556-571.

Israelite, L. (1983). Adult student self-evaluation. *Performance and Instruction, 22* (5), 15-16.

Jaques, E. (1989). *Requisite organization: The CEO's guide to creative structure and leadership.* Arlington, VA: Cason Hall.

Juran, J.M. (1988). *Juran on planning for quality.* New York: Free Press.

Kearsley, B. (1986). Analyzing the costs and benefits of training: Part 2, Identifying the cost and benefits. *Performance and Instruction, 25* (3), 23-25.

King, D.B. (1982). *A correlational analysis of the relationship between selected trainee variables and methods of training course evaluation.*

Unpublished doctoral dissertation, Georgia State University, Atlanta.

Lawton, R.L. (1989, May). Creating a customer-centered culture for service quality. *Quality Progress,* pp. 34-36.

Lewin, K. (1951). *Field theory in social sciences.* New York: Harper & Row.

Lincoln, Y., & Guba, E. (1985). *Naturalistic inquiry.* Newbury Park, CA: Sage.

Lindsey, E.H., Homes, V., & McCall, M.W., Jr. (1987). *Key events in executives' lives.* Greensboro, NC: Center for Creative Leadership.

Martelli, J.T. (1987). Management training: What's it worth? *Performance and Instruction, 26* (9/10), 32-36.

McCall, M.W., Jr., Lombardo, M.M., & Morrison, A.M. (1988). *The lessons of experience.* Lexington, MA: Lexington Books.

Merriam, S.B. (1988). *Case study research in education.* San Francisco: Jossey-Bass.

Miles, W.G., & Biggs, W.D. (1979). Common, recurring and avoidable errors in management development. *Training and Development Journal, 33* (2), 32-35.

Nichol, P. (1989). *Evaluating training for retention.* Unpublished manuscript.

Peters, L.H., & O'Conner, E.J. (1980). Situational constraints and work outcomes: The influence of a frequently overlooked construct. *Academy of Management Review, 5,* 391-397.

Puterbaugh, G., Rosenberg, M., & Sofman, R. (1989). Performance support tools: A step beyond training. *Performance and Instruction, 28* (10), 1-5.

Revans, R.W. (1980). *Action learning.* London: Blonde & Briggs.

Revans, R.W. (1988). *The golden jubilee of action learning.* Manchester, England: University of Manchester, Manchester Business School.

Rightsoft, Inc. (1988). *RightWriter* [computer program].

Rogers, C.A. (1969). *Freedom to learn.* Westerville, OH: Charles E. Merrill.

Rose, A. (1985). *Acquisition and retention of soldiering skills.* Technical Report 671, U. S. Army Research Institute, Alexandria, VA.

Santos, J.L.G. (1989). Participatory action research. *American Behavioral Scientist, 32* (5), 574-581.

Schon, D.A. (1987). *Educating the reflective practitioner.* San Francisco: Jossey-Bass.

Seidel, J.V., & Clark, J.A. (1984). The ethnograph: A computer program for the analysis of qualitative data. *Qualitative Sociology, 7* (1 & 2), 110-125.

Showers, B. (1982). *Transfer of training: The contribution of coaching.* Eugene, OR: University of Oregon, Center of Educational Policy and Management, College of Education.

Soar, R.S., & Soar, R.M. (1982). *Content effects in teaching-learning process.* Unpublished manuscript.

Spencer, L.M. (1983). *Soft skill competencies.* Edinburgh, Scotland: Lindsay.

Spencer, L.M. (1985). Calculating HRD costs and benefits. In W.R. Tracey (Ed.), *Human resources management and development handbook* (pp. 1486-1510). New York: AMACOM.

Sund, R.B. (1976). *Piaget for educators.* Westerville, OH: Charles E. Merrill.

Swanson, R.A., & Gradous, D.B. (1988). *Forecasting financial benefits.* San Francisco: Jossey-Bass.

Vaill, P.B. (1989). *Managing as a performing art.* San Francisco: Jossey-Bass.

Weick, K.E. (1983). Managerial thought in the context of action. In Suresh Srivasta and Associates, *The executive mind* (pp. 221-242). San Francisco: Jossey-Bass.

Wexley, K.N., & Baldwin, T.T. (1986). Posttraining strategies for facilitating positive transfer: An empirical exploration. *Academy of Management Journal, 29* (3), 503- 520.

Whyte, W.F. (Ed.). (1989). Action research for the twenty-first century: Participation, reflection, and practice. *American Behavioral Scientist, 32* (5).

Yelon, S.L., & Berge, Z.L. (1987, May/June). Using fancy checklists for efficient feedback. *Performance and Instruction, 26* (4), 14-20.

Yu, J., & Cooper, H. (1983). A quantitative review of research design effects on response rates to questionnaires. *Journal of Marketing Research, 20* (1), 36-44.

Zemke, R. (1985). The Honeywell studies: How managers learn to manage. *Training: The Magazine of Human Resource Development, 22* (8), 46-51.

Zemke, R., & Kramlinger, T. (1988). *Figuring things out.* Reading, MA: Addison-Wesley.

Index